A217 Introducing religions

Islam

Study Guide

Prepared for the module team by David Herbert
with contributions from Marion Bowman and Hugh Beattie

This publication forms part of the Open University course A217 *Introducing Religions*. Details of this and other Open University courses can be obtained from the Student Registration and Enquiry Service, The Open University, PO Box 197, Milton Keynes, MK7 6BJ, United Kingdom: tel. +44 (0)870 333 4340, email general-enquiries@open.ac.uk

Alternatively, you may visit the Open University website at http://www.open.ac.uk where you can learn more about the wide range of courses and packs offered at all levels by The Open University.

To purchase a selection of Open University course materials visit http://www.ouw.co.uk, or contact Open University Worldwide, Michael Young Building, Walton Hall, Milton Keynes MK7 6AA, United Kingdom for a brochure. tel. +44 (0)1908 858785; fax +44 (0)1908 858787; email ouwenq@open.ac.uk

The Open University
Walton Hall, Milton Keynes
MK7 6AA

First published 2005. Second edition 2012.

Edited and designed by The Open University.

Typeset by The Open University.

Printed in the United Kingdom by TJ International, Padstow.

ISBN 978 1 7800 7412 2

2.1

MIX
Paper from responsible sources
FSC www.fsc.org FSC® C013056

Contents

Introduction 7

Plan of the set text and study guide 7

1 Perceptions and definitions of Islam 10

Defining Islam 11

Thinking about religion: some considerations in relation to Islam 13

Religion and state in Western Europe 15

A brief history of Muslim–Christian encounter 16

2 Experiencing Islam: *hajj* 22

The impact of *hajj*: pilgrims in Mecca 23

The impact of *hajj*: personal perspectives 24

The impact of *hajj*: wall paintings in Egypt 32

Other forms of pilgrimage 33

3 Leadership and law 34

The Islamic state, Islamic civilisation, and Muslim ideas of a 'Golden Age' 35

The spread of Islam and Islamic civilisation 36

The nature of Islamic revival 37

Revival across the Muslim world? The results of a survey 38

Islam and Islamism 46

Alternative views on the social bases of Islamism 46

4 The Qur'an and the Prophet 51

The contents of the Qur'an: a closer look 53

Hearing the Qur'an 57

5 Islamic visual and material culture 73

Calligraphy beyond the page 73

Representational art 73

Depicting the Prophet 76

6 The *Sira* (biography) of Muhammad 78

The new revelation and its relation to past tradition 79

The *hijrah*, and development of relations with Jewish tribes 80

The Prophet in tradition and modernity 82

7 Divine unicity 92

The legacy of the Kharijites: Wahhabism, Saudi Arabia and Islamist extremism 94

Shi'ism: origins and development 94

Further theological developments in the Sunni and Shi'ite traditions, and Sufism 96

Sufism 98

Shi'ism and Iran 109

Islamic unity and diversity in architectural practice: the mosque 110

Geographical diversity in Islam 120

8 *Shari'a* and its consequences 122

Sources of *shari'a* 123

Shari'a and society 125

9 Women, family and gender issues 127

Egyptian and Indonesian attitudes to women, work and child-rearing 129

Marriage, divorce and sexuality 133

Women and gender in a social and political context 134

Islam and feminism 136

Alternative perspectives on women and Islam 138

Male dress in Islam 150

Islamic dress: conclusion 151

10 The two *jihads* 153

Post September 11th reflections 153

11 Islam and Islamism: the future? 168

An alternative perspective on Islamic/Islamist futures 170

Conclusion 175

Bibliography 178

Acknowledgements 180

Materials you will need

The materials for this part of the module comprise:

- Ruthven, M. (2012) *Islam: A Very Short Introduction*, 2nd edn, Oxford: Oxford University Press (set book)
- DVD (all references are to the Islam section of the DVD)
- Audio CD 1

Introduction

Welcome to this introduction to Islam. This study guide will take you through the set book, *Islam: A Very Short Introduction* by Malise Ruthven (2012), augmenting the text with explanation and greater detail and with readings. (These readings are reproduced following the spelling and editorial conventions of their original publication.) You will also be referred to films on the module DVD and tracks 24 to 41 on Audio CD 1.

You will spend the next few weeks studying this material, which will introduce you to the literature, rituals, history and culture that have defined Muslim experience, with a special emphasis on issues facing present-day Muslims and on Islam's place in the contemporary world. This emphasis follows that in the set book by Ruthven (2012). However, since any 'very short introduction' is inevitably selective, the material in this study guide will expand some of the areas that are less well covered by Ruthven: for example, we include a section on art and architecture. This study guide will also introduce some general issues and questions for the study of religion. It will encourage you to think about the different sources of information that you use, and examine issues of perspective and bias. Each tradition studied in A217 focuses on introducing a particular theme or themes. In studying Islam, we will look in particular at the role of women in religion, questions of boundaries between the religious and the secular, and ways of thinking about the relationship between religion and society.

Plan of the set text and study guide

Many introductions to Islam follow a chronological plan, beginning with a study of Muhammad, the final and definitive Prophet of Islam, and then working through the Qur'an (the holy book of Islam) to the early history of the Muslim community, and on through history.

Ruthven's book follows a different plan, beginning instead by examining some of the different interpretations of contemporary Islam and the controversies surrounding them (Chapter 1). In Chapter 2, Ruthven falls in with the more conventional pattern by considering Muhammad and the Qur'an. The rest of the book is arranged thematically. Chapter 3 considers the idea of 'oneness' (*tawhid*) that is central to Islamic thinking, yet reflected in a diversity of ways in Muslim history. Chapter 4 considers *shari'a* (usually translated as 'Islamic law'), which has an important role in Muslim thinking and history. Chapters 5 and 6 consider two issues that have assumed a significant and controversial place in Muslim experience in the modern period: gender, and especially the roles of women, and *jihad* ('struggle' – often translated as 'holy war', but actually having a much broader range of meanings). The conclusion returns to some of the broad issues raised in Chapter 1 concerning Islam's place in the modern world, and an appendix explains the five central ritual practices of Islam – the so-called 'Five Pillars'.

This study guide takes you through Ruthven more or less from beginning to end, changing the order of reading only slightly from time to time within particular chapters. Readings from other sources, illustrations, and references to the DVD and Audio CD are included along the way; questions are set and answers discussed. Please note that we expect that you will need to allocate more than one week for your study of Ruthven's first chapter because it raises many issues.

Meet the author

Before you start reading, you will find it useful and interesting to listen to Malise Ruthven, the author of *Islam: A Very Short Introduction*, in conversation with David Herbert, the author of this study guide, on Audio CD 1, tracks 25 to 34. Listen to the whole conversation, pausing to take notes, reflect, or go over any difficult parts as you wish, but not worrying too much about grasping every detail at this stage. You will be asked to review the conversation in the conclusion to this study guide, and you will find it useful to refer to the interview at various points as specific issues discussed in it crop up in your reading of *Islam: A Very Short Introduction*. As you listen to the interview, you may find the following questions useful to help you to engage with the conversation.

EXERCISE

1 What concerns does Ruthven express about the use of the term 'fundamentalism' to describe movements within Islam, and why does he favour the use of the term 'religious nationalism'?

2 Why was the picture depicting Muhammad dropped from *Islam: A Very Short Introduction*?

3 Why does Ruthven think that Sufism has been such an important influence on the development of Islamic tradition in so many different contexts?

4 How does Ruthven respond to Samuel Huntingdon's argument in 'The clash of civilisations' (1993) that, after the Cold War, the West faces a new civilisation threat in the Islamic world?

5 What does Ruthven see as being the long-term impact of 'September 11th' (the al-Qaeda attack on the World Trade Centre) on Islam?

DISCUSSION

1 Ruthven argues that if 'fundamentalism' is taken in the sense in which it was originally developed, to describe Christian groups who believe in the literal inspiration of scripture, then it is not a useful term to discriminate between different groups of Muslims, because nearly all Muslims believe in the literal inspiration of the Qur'an. Also, 'fundamentalism' is often applied to Islam to describe groups that take a politically militant stance, which most Muslims do not share. Therefore, Ruthven thinks that 'religious nationalism' is a better term to describe such movements.

2 The picture of Muhammad was dropped because of an email campaign directed at the publishers. They discussed its inclusion with Ruthven who agreed to its removal. Ruthven's later comments shed some light on why there is strong sensitivity to this issue among some contemporary Muslims.

3 Two main reasons are mentioned. First, Sufism provided an organisational structure for the transmission of Islamic tradition in the absence of any strong central religious authorities. Secondly, Sufism's emphasis on inner spirituality and the development of the self has a broad appeal, including in secular environments, of which Ruthven gives the example of white converts in the USA.

4 Ruthven rejects the idea of a clash of civilisations between Islam and the West, but argues that historical experience across cultures shaped by a religion can have significant consequences, giving the example of the prohibition of images of living beings as a form of idolatry (*shirk*) in Islam. This has meant that the great proliferation of images in the electronic age has been particularly challenging for many traditional Muslim societies, and for migrants coming to the West from such societies. This, perhaps, includes the reaction to the picture of Muhammad that was dropped from *Islam: A Very Short Introduction*. However, as we shall see in the exercises on Muslim material culture, visual culture – including some representational art – has a long tradition in some parts of the Muslim world.

5 Ruthven thinks that the long-term effects of September 11th are likely to be a further reaction against militant political Islam among the majority of Muslims, combined with the development of forms of Islam compatible with 'pluralism', which means the coexistence of a range of religious traditions within a society, among which people may choose or not choose without compulsion. □

1
Perceptions and definitions of Islam

This section begins with contemporary views of Islam, and then moves on to problems of defining 'Islam'.

EXERCISE

Jot down a list of ten words, images or associations that spring to mind when you think of the word 'Islam'. We will come back to this list towards the end of the section, to see how your initial perceptions compare with those you form after reading this material.

Read Ruthven, Chapter 1, pages 1 to 7, up to the subheading 'Islam as identity'.

Consider the following questions as you read:

1 What associations does Ruthven suggest are commonly linked with Islam in the media?

2 What alternative associations does he suggest, and why do these tend not to be well represented in the media?

3 What consequences do public perceptions have?

DISCUSSION

1 Islam is often linked in the media with violence and militancy, and this association has been reinforced by more violent incidents involving groups that claim to be Islamic. These include the attacks on New York and Washington by al-Qaeda in September 2001, the bombing of a nightclub in Bali in 2002, the train bombing in Madrid in March 2004, the tube and bus bombings in London in 2005 and the aftermath of the American-led invasion of Iraq in March 2003.

2 Ruthven suggests that these violent images are at odds with the experience of most Muslims, whose daily life associates Islam with self-giving and peace – for example, in the greeting *as salaam 'alaikum* ('peace be upon you'). Part of the problem seems to be that violence gets more media coverage than peace or reconstruction.

3 The problem with the preference for the sensational in media coverage is that impressions of violence – in this case associated with Islam – may then feed back into policy-making processes. ☐

Defining Islam

In one sense defining Islam is a fairly straightforward task – compared with that of defining some other religions. For example, the name 'Hinduism' was given to Indian religious traditions by external invaders (initially Persians, later British), not one that originated on the Indian subcontinent. In contrast, the term 'Islam' was used by Muhammad and his earliest followers to mean 'submission' or 'resignation' (Qur'an, surah 6:125, 39:23). However, there is disagreement among scholars as to whether the 'submission' referred to in the Qur'an is submission to the will of God in general, or to the religion of Muhammad in particular, and hence about the extent to which Islam was initially seen as a different religion from other monotheistic traditions (such as Judaism and Christianity) present in the Arabian peninsula in the first half of the seventh century CE (Sherif, 1995, 117–9; Rippin, 1990, 3–4). Most Muslims assume that the religion of Muhammad was seen as distinct from the beginning of Muhammad's ministry.

A Muslim is someone who declares the *shahada* – the first 'Pillar' (or 'duty') of Islam: 'There is no God but God and Muhammad is his Prophet.' This declaration is shared by roughly 90 per cent of the world's Muslims (Sunni Muslims), and even the other 10 per cent (Shi'ite Muslims) use almost the same declaration, but add a phrase referring to 'Ali (Muhammad's cousin and son-in-law, who is central to Shi'a tradition) as 'the friend of God'. Islam, then, is the tradition to which those who make this declaration belong. The declaration implies recognition of the Qur'an, the revelation of God given via Muhammad, as the final and definitive revelation of God. To properly fulfil the commitment implied in this declaration there are four further basic duties to God (*ibadat*) that the Muslim must perform. These duties are *salat* ('prayer' or 'worship'); *zakat* (giving a prescribed amount of one's wealth to charity); *sawm* (fasting during the month of Ramadan); and *hajj* (pilgrimage to Mecca in Saudi Arabia, which must be done at least once in a lifetime). More details about the five basic duties (often called 'pillars') are given in the appendix to Ruthven (2012, 159–63), but the following gives a basic orientation.

Salat refers to a daily act of worship that must be performed five times, involving precise acts of bowing, kneeling, prostration and recitation while facing the direction of the Ka'ba (a cube-shaped shrine) in Mecca (Saudi Arabia). Ritual washing must be performed before *salat*.

EXERCISE

On the DVD there are examples of *salat* being practised in different places around the world, and you can see the required ritual process step by step. Consider the following questions:

1. In which direction is *salat* performed?
2. Why do you think washing might be so important as an element of preparation for *salat*? (Note: the DVD sequence does not answer this question.)
3. What beliefs are embodied in the performance of *salat*?

DISCUSSION

1. *Salat* is performed in the direction of Mecca (sometimes written as 'Makkah').
2. You might have thought of several reasons, and there is no one right answer. Perhaps through washing the believer may be preparing him/herself to worship God; washing is often a sign of purification. Possibly through the ritual of washing the believer is creating a boundary around the ritual of *salat*, marking it off as special and sacred. You might have thought of more practical reasons – such as making collective prayer a more pleasant experience, especially in a hot climate.
3. The words of *salat* are of praise to God, expressing thankfulness to God as creator, seeking guidance on the straight path of good deeds and avoiding hurting other people. By touching one's nose and forehead on the ground, one acknowledges the greatness of God. Finally, a greeting of peace to the angels on one's right and left shoulders recording one's good and bad deeds in the book of life serves as a reminder of individual responsibility for one's deeds, for which each person will have to account on judgement day. □

Zakat is a kind of religious tax which is used to support the poor in the Muslim community and missionary work (*dawa*). It is set at 2.5 per cent each year of what a person owns (capital assets) above an agreed minimum. There are debates as to whether it should be collected by the state or by religious associations.

Sawm is a fast conducted from dawn until dusk during the ninth month of the Islamic calendar, Ramadan. It requires abstention from food, drink, smoking and sex during daylight hours. As Islam has spread around the world, this has become particularly challenging in locations in the far north, such as Norway, Canada and the Shetland Islands, where daylight hours in the summer months are very long. However, Muslims living above the Arctic Circle are allowed to use the standard hours of sunrise/sunset in Mecca.

Hajj is a pilgrimage to Mecca that involves performing a set of rituals over ten days during the twelfth month of the Islamic calendar. The rituals of *hajj* are illustrated on the DVD, and I shall ask you to look at the film in detail later. *Hajj* is required to be performed once in a person's lifetime if possible, and has often been performed at great expense and sacrifice in terms of hardship, effort, cost and time, especially in eras when transport was much more difficult than it is now. Even today, the journey is often a great sacrifice for poor pilgrims. The *hajj* is of great symbolic significance – an illustration of the unity of Islam and unity of humanity before God. Pilgrims from all corners of the world gather in one place and, regardless of wealth, culture or colour, wear the same simple white robes. Physically arduous as well as a time for reflection, the experience has been a turning point in many pilgrims' lives. For example, after taking part in *hajj* alongside people of all colours, the black American political activist Malcolm X abandoned a racially exclusive version of Islam that had developed in reaction to conditions of discrimination in the USA in the 1950s and 1960s. The end of *hajj* is marked by a great feast celebrated not just by pilgrims (*hajjis*; female *hajjas*) in Mecca, but across the Muslim world, and known as *'Id al-Adha* (the Feast of the Sacrifice) in Arabic, or *Bayram* in Turkish.

The other duties that follow from the commitment to be a Muslim are called *muamalat*, and refer to obligations to others and to oneself. These are worked out in the *shari'a* (Islamic law, but the word originally means 'path' or 'way'), which is compiled from several sources including the *Qur'an* and the *hadiths* ('traditions' – reports or anecdotes of Muhammad's actions and sayings). The *shari'a* lays out what is forbidden (*haram*) and what is permitted (*halal* – as in *halal* butchers, who sell meat slaughtered in an Islamically acceptable way). There are five major historic schools for the interpretation of *shari'a* (four *Sunni* and one *Shi'ite*), and many more differences of opinion about the meaning of *shari'a* today.

Thinking about religion: some considerations in relation to Islam

Before reading Ruthven (2012), pages 7 to 14, it is worth pausing briefly to consider different understandings of the definition and scope of the terms 'religion' and 'Islam'. First, consider this quotation by the late Palestinian (and Christian) writer Edward Said:

> At present, Islam and the West have taken on a powerful new urgency everywhere. And we must note immediately that it is always the West, not Christianity, that seems pitted against Islam.

> Why? Because the assumption is that whereas 'the West' is greater than and has surpassed the stage of Christianity, its principal religion, the world of Islam – its varied societies, histories, and languages notwithstanding – is still mired in religion, primitiveness and backwardness. Therefore the West is modern, greater than the sum of its parts, full of enriching contradictions and yet always Western in its cultural identity; the world of Islam, on the other hand, is no more than 'Islam', reducible to a small number of unchanging characteristics and experiences that seem on the surface to be as plentiful as the West.
>
> (Said, 1997, 10–11)

As we have seen by looking at the Five Pillars, at its core Islamic belief is fairly straightforward. The main obligations to God are clearly defined, and the major sources from which *shari'a* is derived are widely agreed upon, although the detail of their interpretation varies. But the extent to which the term 'Islam' is also appropriately used to describe the broader culture of Muslim-majority societies is disputed, as the above quotation illustrates. Said suggests here that 'Islam' is used by Westerners to include 'varied societies, histories, and languages'. The implication of Westerners using the term 'Islam' in this broad way is negative, Said claims, because societies in which religion still has a large influence are viewed as 'backward', places where areas of social life have not yet obtained the kind of freedom from religious domination that characterises the contemporary West.

However, the term 'Islam' is used in this broad sense by some Muslims with a positive meaning, because they see the reduction of religious influence in many areas of Western societies as a negative development, and wish to see religion restored to its central place in society, often through the wider application of *shari'a*. Such Muslims are sometimes called 'Islamists'. One recent scholar defined an Islamist as: 'a Muslim who regards Islam as a body of ideas, values, beliefs and practices encompassing all spheres of life, including personal and social relationships, economics and politics' (Roald, 2001, xii).

In fact, followers of many religious traditions claim that their faith has the kinds of wider implications described here. However, it is probably fair to say that, taken globally, in the last thirty-five years (since 1970) Islamist movements have been among the most prominent groups to attempt to assert the importance of religion in politics and society.

There are thus debates between some Western critics of Islam (as portrayed by Said) and Islamists over the 'proper' scope and place of 'religion', and hence it will be helpful to consider briefly the history of how 'religion' has come to be understood in many European societies, and how Christian-majority European societies have interacted with Muslim-majority societies through history and up to the present.

Religion and state in Western Europe

The term 'religion', now used globally, has been decisively shaped by its use in post-Christian cultures (King, 1999). After bitter religious wars between Christians (Catholics in opposition to Protestants and vice versa, and struggles between various Protestant groups) during the sixteenth and seventeenth centuries in Christian-majority Europe, the idea developed of separating religion from politics by creating a secular public realm, free from religious influence:

> For a long time, Catholics and Protestants shared the view that only one of their creeds could survive. This meant that one had to destroy the other, and they differed only on which one it should be. ... Certain people ... saw a possibility of approaching the problem differently, so that this kind of question would not arise. They proposed finding a way to view this disagreement as a normal one, containable within the scope of a decent human life. Their work made it possible for toleration to be developed without the fearful sense of betrayal which it had seemed at first to involve.
>
> (Midgley, 1989, 242)

This new understanding eventually enabled Western Christian societies to become (on the whole) much more tolerant of religious diversity – although one should remember how long this took (Catholics could not become members of Parliament in the United Kingdom until the Catholic Emancipation Act of 1829), and how such divisions continue to have political importance in some places. (It should also be noted that the connection between religion and the state generally remained stronger in countries where Orthodox Christianity is the majority religion, for example, Greece and Russia.)

All this is relevant because this new way of containing religious difference occurred at a time when European powers were beginning to extend their influence beyond Europe. As they did so, not least into the Muslim-majority world, they brought with them an understanding of the separation of religion from politics in a form that did not exist prior to European colonial influence. Furthermore, in eighteenth-century Europe the intellectual movement known as the Enlightenment produced a way of thinking that made possible for the first time the study of religion from an 'outsider' perspective – as a cultural object or system – rather than from an 'insider' perspective – as the subject of devotion or authority. These cultural developments arrived in the Muslim-majority world with colonial administrators and emissaries from European powers, who brought with them new and alien understandings of religion and of religion's place in society, and varying amounts of power, influence and will to impose them.

A brief history of Muslim–Christian encounter

This brings us to the second very short history that can help us understand why the scope of the terms 'religion' and 'Islam' is disputed in contemporary religious and Islamic studies (and beyond): the history of Muslim–Christian encounter. There had been competition between rival Muslim and Christian empires since Muslim armies expanded west and north from Arabia in the mid-seventh century. Between the eleventh and thirteenth centuries CE, Western European Christian armies conducted crusades to recapture and guarantee access to Christian holy sites in Palestine. Between the eighth and thirteenth centuries much of Spain was Muslim territory, the last Muslim outpost, Granada, surviving until 1492. From the fifteenth to the later nineteenth centuries the Balkans were mostly ruled by the Muslim Ottoman empire. As a result Muslims are the outright majority in Albania and Kosovo today, the largest religious community in Bosnia, and a major minority in Macedonia. So terms such as 'Christian-majority' Europe are only approximate generalisations, and using the term 'majority' reminds us that both Muslim-majority and Christian- (or post-Christian) majority societies contain significant minorities of other religious groups.

This history of imperial rivalries has shaped attitudes in the Muslim-majority and Christian-majority worlds, and antagonisms have often been exacerbated by the European colonisation of some Muslim-majority societies, colonial encroachment on others, and a post-colonial history that has seen Muslim-majority societies used as pawns in the Cold War struggle between the USA and the USSR, American support for Israel (seen by many in the Muslim-majority world as an attack on the Muslim-majority Palestinian population), and continued European and American intervention in the Middle East, including the two Gulf Wars (1991 and 2003).

Unsurprisingly, given this turbulent history, Western ideas, including secularism and the notion of a detached, critical study of religion, are viewed with suspicion by many in the Muslim-majority world. Religion has tended to remain much more of an integrated part of life in Muslim-majority societies than in many Christian or post-Christian societies, and hence the division between 'religious' and 'secular' fits uneasily with an Islamic conception of obligations to God and of *sharī'a* as encompassing all of life. Islamic ideas and practices permeate everyday life for its followers – how people eat, wash, marry, conduct their family and

Figure 1 The Sultan Ahmet (Blue) Mosque, Istanbul, Turkey, built by Mehmet Aga 1609–17. The style of this mosque was influenced by St Sophia, the great imperial Christian church in Constantinople that was converted into a mosque. Photo: © Sonia Halliday Photographs.

personal relationships – such that religion is an integral part of the culture. This culture may be quite flexible in practice and is certainly subject to change over time, but it also forms part of the background against which family and personal decisions are taken.

Furthermore, in some Muslim-majority societies, conformity to aspects of Islam is required by the law of the land, not just as a matter of cultural custom or religious duty which might be rejected without legal sanction (though often at a high social cost), but actually legally enforced – for example, the prohibition on the sale of alcohol, or severe penalties for adultery (stoning to death), in Saudi Arabia. However, while some (especially Islamists) argue that Islam ought to be reflected in the law and government of a country, others strongly reject this position.

Finally, it is important to remember that distinctions between 'Islam' and 'the West' are at best only crude generalisations. Many Muslims now live in Western countries (an estimated ten to twelve million in each of the USA and Western Europe), and there is often a long history of settlement going back centuries, although mass migration has mostly taken place since 1950. Also, as we have seen, European influence in the Muslim-majority world goes back several centuries, and has been intense in many areas since 1800, so that many Muslims share the secular outlooks that have become popular among Europeans and more broadly in the West.

EXERCISE

Consider the following questions:

1. Who is a Muslim, and what characteristics define the Islamic way of life?
2. What disagreements have arisen over the scope and nature of religion – and in particular Islam – in the modern era?

DISCUSSION

1. A Muslim is someone who declares the *shahada*. The Muslim way of life is characterised by following the Five Pillars (*shahada*, 'declaration'; *salat*, 'prayer/worship'; *zakat*, 'contribution (to good works)'; *sawm*, fasting in Ramadan; and *hajj*, pilgrimage to Mecca – and by seeking to live according to *shari'a*.
2. Disagreements have arisen because although some Westerners regard religion either as 'primitive' or purely a matter of personal choice, many Muslims (along with some followers of other religions) insist that Islam permeates all areas of life. This may be asserted in an ideological way, but also in practice, because Islam is part of the culture of everyday life for many Muslims. Some currents in European thought, as the quotations from Said and Midgley suggest, see this pervasiveness of religion in everyday life as a sign of backwardness. □

EXERCISE

Now read Ruthven, 'Islam as identity', pages 7 to 9, and consider the following questions:

1. Why has the term 'Muslim' become a mark of identity in some situations?
2. Can you think of other situations where Islam has become an important mark of identity?

DISCUSSION

1 Ruthven writes that the term 'Muslim' sometimes becomes a marker of identity to distinguish between people of different groups – for example, 'Muslim' from Serb (Christian, Orthodox) or from Croat (Christian, Catholic) in the former Yugoslavia. As elsewhere in the former communist world, this designation may have little to do with personal belief or practice, especially given the impact of many years of communist rule on the transmission of religious traditions.

2 Islam has also become a mark of identity in situations where Muslims have migrated from Muslim-majority societies to minority situations, and where their religion has sometimes become a new source of pride, community cohesion and means of adaptation to new environments, which may be experienced as difficult or hostile. □

Now read Ruthven, 'Islam as political ideology', pages 9 to 12. Ruthven does not actually define what he means by 'political ideology', so before reading this section it is worth pausing to think about this term. It may be defined simply as 'a system of political thought'. However, it is sometimes used in a more specific sense. The *Concise Oxford Dictionary* defines the current use of 'ideology' as a 'manner of thinking characteristic of a class or individual, ideas at the basis of some economic or political theory or system'. In sociology the term is used to refer to the idea that ways of thinking are formed by the historical experience of a group, especially by the social and economic position occupied by that group. Sometimes this is seen in a 'deterministic' way: that people's ideas are so shaped by their social status and economic position that they are incapable of thinking 'outside the box' – their thoughts directly reflect their social position. As we shall see, this kind of argument is sometimes used to 'explain' the political uses of contemporary Islam. However, while social and economic circumstances undoubtedly influence how people think about things, we should be careful not to over-simplify the relationship between thinking and circumstances, as people in similar circumstances often think very differently.

EXERCISE

1 Where and when did the term 'fundamentalism' originate, and what are the differences between the Christian and Muslim groups to whom this term has been applied?

2 What criticisms have been made of modern movements that seek an 'Islamic state'?

3 Why does Ruthven argue that fundamentalism is not an appropriate term to describe Muslim groups?

DISCUSSION

1 The term 'fundamentalist' was first used to refer to an American Protestant movement at the beginning of the twentieth century. This was a protest movement that objected to the spread of ideas and methods in theological training colleges which questioned the historical or literal truth of the Bible. Instead, they sought a return to what they saw as the 'fundamentals' of Christian belief – such as the literal truth of the six-day creation account, the virgin birth and physical resurrection of Jesus, and the imminent return of Christ. In contrast, the term has mainly been applied to Muslims who seek 'to restore or establish an Islamic state' (Ruthven, 2012, 9).

The term 'fundamentalist' is a contested term and commentators disagree about its meaning. It will be examined in more detail later. A key point for now is that when used of Muslims, the term 'fundamentalist' mainly describes groups with political aspirations, whereas in a Christian context the focus is on beliefs. This is partly because most Muslims are 'fundamentalist' in their approach to scripture, since 'virtually all believing Muslims ... see the Quran as the eternal unmediated Word of God' (Ruthven, 2012, 9). In contrast, the idea that Islam ought to determine the form of the modern state is controversial among Muslims.

2 Two main criticisms are highlighted here. First, the idea of an Islamic state is usually defined in terms of the implementation of *shari'a*. Against this, critics point out that, in Muslim history, societies have never been 'governed exclusively according to Islamic law' (Ruthven, 2012, 10). This is because other powers and institutions have always been present – for example, local customs and alternative court systems. A further argument that could be made is that *shari'a* cannot simply be implemented, because it is not a straightforward legal system. Rather, it consists of various elements whose interpretation has always been disputed between different commentators. We shall come back to this point.

Secondly, critics argue that the founders of modern political Islam do not really return to some pristine original Islam, but actually incorporate all kinds of modern elements in their teachings. Ruthven points to the impact of fascist thought on Maududi, and of existentialist thought on Qutb. Both these (i.e. existentialism and fascism) were movements of modern European origin.

3 First, it seems that fundamentalism may not be a suitable term for describing political Islam because it carries with it from its Christian origins the idea of a return to the basics of religious belief, whereas in Islam it has mostly been used for groups who have political ambitions. Secondly, using the term seems to concede to the political

militants that their interpretation of Islam as a political ideology is indeed the fundamental or original one, whereas this interpretation is strongly contested among Muslims. □

Now read Ruthven, 'Islam as faith', pages 12 to 14.

EXERCISE

1 What is the difference between *islam* and *iman*?

2 What did the Kharijis believe, and how did the Murji'ites disagree? What long-term consequences has the defeat of the Khariji view had? (Note: the historical context of this dispute is considered more fully in the commentary on Ruthven, Chapter 2 below. The issues to note here are the basic point of disagreement, and the long-term consequences of this dispute.)

DISCUSSION

1 The term '*islam*' refers to the outward profession of faith, *iman* to the inward or spiritual dimension of faith. Ruthven uses an incident from the Qur'an to illustrate the point: a group of Bedouin (nomadic) Arabs had made a public confession of faith, but '[true] faith ha[d] not yet entered [their] hearts' (Qur'an 49:14; Ruthven, 2012, 12).

2 The Kharijis believed that 'grave sinners' (Ruthven, 2012, 12) could not be considered Muslims at all, whereas the Murji'ites argued that anyone who publicly makes the confession of faith (the *shahada*: 'There is no God but God; Muhammad is the Messenger of God') should be considered a Muslim, even if they have lapsed in practice. Arguably, the victory of the Murji'ites has had long-term consequences in Islamic history, because it meant that the majority Sunni community has not become divided over theological issues, and that Muslim communities over the centuries have been relatively tolerant about differences of belief. □

However, this is not to say that there is not significant diversity of belief and practice in Islam. Later we shall look at some of the differences that have developed between the majority Sunni and minority Shi'ite Muslim communities, and, among Sunnis, between the Sufis, who follow a more inwardly focused or mystical form of Islam, and the '*ulama* or legal scholars, who are more concerned with conformity of practice.

2
Experiencing Islam: *hajj*

Although the relationship between Islam and politics is a central one in the contemporary world, it is also important to balance this by looking at personal experiences of being a Muslim. One of the highlights of a Muslim's life is the obligation to go on *hajj*, pilgrimage to Mecca, at least once in a lifetime, if at all possible. In the following sections we will examine the DVD material on the experience of Muslims going on *hajj*, which shows some of the main rituals and includes some discussion of what this all meant to the participants. We shall also read two personal accounts by pilgrims from different parts of the world – Tartarstan (a former Soviet republic) and South Africa. Finally we shall look at the way some Egyptian pilgrims record and celebrate their *hajj* experiences by painting scenes on the walls of their houses.

Figure 2 Photography by Adrees Latif. Nearly one million pilgrims face the Ka'ba in prayer at the Grand Mosque in Mecca during sunset, 27 February 2001. Photo: © Reuters/CORBIS.

The impact of *hajj*: pilgrims in Mecca

EXERCISE

The film on the DVD follows UK pilgrims from different ethnic backgrounds going on *hajj* for the first time. You should now view the *hajj* film and consider the following questions.

1 What are the rituals that pilgrims perform?

2 What do they say about their experiences?

DISCUSSION

Please note that not all the following details are shown on the DVD; the additional information is provided below to enhance your understanding of the rituals.

1 On arrival in Mecca many pilgrims perform the *'umra*, or 'lesser pilgrimage'. This can be performed at any time of year, but is often added on to the beginning or end of *hajj*, the 'greater pilgrimage'. *'Umra* involves performing *salat* at the Great Mosque in Mecca, and then circumambulating (walking around) the Ka'ba, the cube-shaped shrine in the centre of the Great Mosque, seven times. The Ka'ba is the site where, according to Muslim tradition, Ibrahim offered to sacrifice Isma'il to Allah. Jewish and Muslim traditions both trace the origins of their covenant with God to Ibrahim (Abraham in Jewish traditions), but through different sons – Isma'il (Ishmael) in Muslim tradition, Isaac in Jewish tradition. The next stage of *'umra* is to move as fast as possible seven times between two small hills, Safa and Marwa, imitating the search of Isma'il's mother, Hagar, for water to feed the infant Isma'il. This completes the *'umra*.

The *hajj* proper begins on the eighth day of the Islamic month Dhu'l-Hijja, where, after a ritual of purification, the pilgrims leave Mecca for the tent-city of Mina, five miles away. They stay there overnight, and the next morning make their way to the plain of 'Arafat, some ten miles away, assembling on the Mount of Mercy, where a period of reflection and repentance takes place from midday to dusk. Pilgrims return to Muzdalifa, about half-way back to Mina, to spend the night. The next day they return to Mina and stone a pillar, which represents Shaitan (Satan). This is followed by the ritual slaughter of goats and sheep in the festival of *'Id al-Adha* (Feast of the Sacrifice), which is also celebrated at the same time by Muslims across the world. This marks the climax of the *hajj*. The pilgrims then return to Mecca, and those pilgrims who did not complete the *'umra* prior to *hajj* perform the *'umra* rituals. At this stage, ritual purity is abandoned, symbolised by men having their heads shaved, and women a lock of their hair cut off. This marks the official end of the pilgrimage, but for most pilgrims there follow three days of feasting in Mina, during which time the pillar representing Shaitan will again be stoned (and two other pillars are stoned as well), and the Ka'ba is again circumambulated. Many pilgrims also visit Medina, the city where the Prophet first established a Muslim community as its ruler, before returning home.

2 Pilgrims report how the experience of going on *hajj* exceeds their expectations, especially the impact of being among so many fellow Muslims. Ascending the Mount of Mercy, the experience of collective repentance and sense of purification is profoundly moving for some. Others reflect a certain surprise at some aspects of the experience that are perhaps more distant from their home experience – such as the stoning of the pillar at Mina, or the rather haphazard organisation – yet a sense of profound togetherness and renewed spirituality seems to be the overall impression. □

The impact of *hajj*: personal perspectives

The following are two, rather different, accounts of experiencing *hajj*. In the first reading, Gÿlnar Baltanova, a female Muslim university lecturer from Tartarstan in the former Soviet Union, reflects on her experiences of travelling to Mecca to perform the *hajj* with her father in 1993, and then '*umra* with her mother in 1995.

READING 1

Mecca

Uniting in a single belief

I had read a lot about the *hajj*, its rituals, obligations, and prohibitions. But because of the lack of information about the very few people who had journeyed to Mecca from Communist Russia, I had some misconceptions. One of these was that it was forbidden for women. I never dreamed that I would be able to perform it twice: first, the *hajj* proper with my father in 1993, and then the *Umrah* (little pilgrimage) with my mother in 1995.

This second pilgrimage was both the more interesting journey and the more meritorious from the Muslim point of view. We performed it during Ramadan, the season of fasting, and were told by our Imam that *Umrah* during Ramadan is equivalent to the pilgrimage made with the prophet Muhammad. We traveled from Kazan by bus, a journey of more than nine days of nonstop driving and fasting. We crossed

Western Russia, Ukraine, Romania, Bulgaria, Turkey, Syria, Jordan, and part of Saudi Arabia without the comforts of long stops, hotels, or hot meals.

The first group of pilgrims (men only) from Tartarstan had journeyed to Mecca in 1992. The following year, my father and I joined a group of 170 pilgrims from Tartarsan and several other republics of the former USSR. Everything was new to us! We had been raised under the banner of state atheism and lived in a secular society in which no distinctions existed in any sphere of life between men and women. We were accustomed to having independence and the freedom to make our own decisions.

Thus, for most of us, the *hajj* came as a culture shock. It was our first experience of the fully fledged Muslim way of life, and many of us were unprepared. To start with, although views differ on this question, most modern Islamic scholars insist that women participating in the *hajj* must be accompanied by either their husbands or a close male relative – father, brother, or son. For Russian women, this rule proved very difficult: Many are single, and as the journey is expensive, few families can afford to send more than one member on the pilgrimage.

This rule is not without good reason: The *hajj* is very strenuous physically. For instance, women are permitted to approach and kiss the black stone of the Ka'ba, but in the overcrowded mosque, it is often physically impossible for a woman to do so. Moreover, some rituals can only be performed by men. For example, the *Talbiya* (sacred formula) has to be spoken aloud, but women are not permitted to speak in the presence of strange men.

When we started our journey, given our preconceptions, we were surprised to find that nearly half of our group were women. We were even more surprised to discover that women constitute half of all pilgrims on the *hajj*. We were amazed, too, to see how many young pilgrims there were, since the *hajj* is traditionally performed by older people.

The *hajj* begins with entering the state of *ihram* (ritual purity), which has both a spiritual and material aspect. For women, *ihram* means wearing a long white dress and a veil covering the head. Nothing must emphasize the women's figure: In fact, she must hide her age, beauty, and physical merits. Any man in the street is entitled to upbraid her if she infringes this rule.

Despite the difficulties and the patience needed to complete the rituals, the *hajj* gave us a unique religious experience. Nothing in the world can compare with the atmosphere in Mecca, with its sea of people dressed in white, with tears in their eyes, all directing their thoughts towards a common goal. Coming from a society in which religion is synonymous with backwardness and ignorance, being part of the three million pilgrims in Mecca, seeing faces filled with passion, ecstasy, and exultation, and meeting people from all over the world united in one belief, was a truly extraordinary experience.

Source: Gÿlnar R. Baltanova, 'Mecca', in Jennifer Westwood (ed.) On Pilgrimage: Sacred Journeys around the World *(Mahwah, New Jersey: HiddenSpring, 2003), 8–10.*

EXERCISE

1 In what ways had being brought up in a communist regime influenced Baltanova's knowledge, expectations and experience of the *hajj*?

2 What seems to have struck Baltanova most about the experience?

DISCUSSION

1 Originally Baltanova had not realised women were allowed on *hajj*, and hence was surprised to find that half of the participants were women. For a woman brought up in the former USSR, the gender dynamics of a Muslim-majority society were unfamiliar and seemed rather restricting. Initially the requirement that women be accompanied by a male relative seemed strange, expensive and impractical, but reasons for this became clearer as she experienced the physical rigours and ritual requirements of *hajj*.

2 Baltanova writes that the atmosphere was unique and highly affirming, especially given the negative view of religion under the Soviet system. The sense of unity and common purpose seems to have been particularly moving. □

The second reading is by Farid Esack, a South African Muslim, academic and journalist. This passage comes from the first chapter of his book, *On Being a Muslim* (1999), although the article first appeared in *Worldview*, the magazine of the Muslim Students Association at the University of Cape Town, in August 1985. At this time the apartheid system was still in place, and very much present in Esack's thoughts as he performed the *hajj* rituals. The Muslim community in South Africa originally came from the Indian subcontinent in the nineteenth century, and maintains close links with India and Pakistan.

On being with Allah

READING 2

Pepsi shows the way

Mecca is referred to in the Qur'an as the *ma'ad*, the place of return (Q. 28:85). I had undertaken my first journey there some years ago and it was meant to be a journey 'home' before the ultimate journey 'home' (the Qur'an also describes all of life as part of this return to Allah, e.g., Q. 2:285; 3:38). For Muslims, a journey to Mecca is also an encounter with our roots; genealogical, religious and spiritual. It is in some ways a return to our genealogical roots because Adam and Eve (Peace be upon them) dwelt on the plains of the Mountain of 'Arafah, located there, after their departure from Paradise. It is a return to our religious roots because the Cave of Hira', where the Prophet Muhammad (Peace be upon him) encountered his first revelation, is the physical point of the beginning of Islam as a religion. Lastly, it is a return to our spiritual roots, because the Ka'bah is the symbol of the presence of Allah, the House of Allah.

I approached Mecca with a mixture of feelings. Social conditioning: the many tales of experiences of 'hearts overflowing' told by returning pilgrims compelling me to just 'feel the greatness of the moment'; my secular disposition militating against this and beckoning me to be calm; the *nafs al-lawwamah* (berating self) mockingly chiding: 'Are you not ashamed of defiling the sacred soil of Mecca with your footprints?' Anyway, the journey had cost a good few hundred dollars and no taunts from a berating self were going to make me turn back.

One actually descends into the *haram* (sacred area) from the barren surrounding hills. And here the Ka'bah rose in its full majesty and glory. If only I, too, I thought, could descend into a seemingly barren self and cause a new being to come forth from a desolate soul. As Muhammad Iqbal, the Pakistani poet, said: 'Re-chisel then your ancient frame and build up a new being – such being, being real being, or else your ego is a mere ring of smoke.' I hoped again for the first time in many years. If this land in its barrenness can become the spring where so much of humankind come to be nourished, then there must be hope. A spring can yet flow from my existence of seeming nothingness and allow me to drink from it, so that I may become fully human and fully Muslim.

Clad in *ihram*, the simple two-piece cotton wrapping worn by all pilgrims, a money bag tied to my waist, my soul tied to the travellers' cheques and my physical body to my passport therein, I joined the multitude in approaching the *bait al-atiq* (ancient house). I became lost in the crowd. Is there then just no limit to the times that one can get lost? Getting lost to intellectual jargon, hobbies, organizations, causes, one's family, even to one's self? Will I ever be found and returned to 'its rightful owner'? Just this once – answer me! I won't ask any more questions after this! (Silence.)

Clinging to my booklet of *du'as* (prayers) I hurriedly completed the seven *tawafs* (circumambulations) around the Ka'bah, dutifully reciting the prescribed *du'a* for each particular round. However desperately needed, there was still no self-expression or erratic, even frenzied, crying from a mutilated self. Was my soul the victim of a conspiracy between the 'ulama (clergy) and that book vendor who sold me this collection of prescribed litanies? Was the written word again going to be the separating wall between me and my Sustainer? Was the eternal alliance between religion and capitalism being replayed here, destroying the innocent and vulnerable?

I was desperate to get the preliminaries over before reaching the Hajar-al-Aswad (Black Stone), a stone reportedly from heaven and placed in that spot by Muhammad, and then ultimately the *multazam*, the door of the Ka'bah. Before I knew it, my first set of circumambulations around the Ka'bah was complete – the first part of an emptying process, a burning out while rotating around the candle before being consumed by the flame. (Was I also following the advice of Jalal al-Din Rumi, who said: 'die before you die', even as I was returning to my place of return, Mecca, before my ultimate return to my Lord?)

I elbowed my way to the Black Stone, fervently hoping that it might absorb my blackness (this was long before I wondered about the equation of sin with blackness), my burdensome title, power games, politico-religious position, eloquence and mess-ups. And then, still clinging to my book of litanies, money bag and passport, I reached the door. Somewhere, something arose from deep within me to destroy the conspiracy between the book vendor and the clergy which demanded that I respond from a prescribed text, and between the modernists and capitalists which demanded that I 'control my emotions'. Temporarily liberated, I lowered my small book and my orderly litanies gave way to uncontrolled weeping. And I remembered the anecdotes of returning South African pilgrims: 'Oh, you should have seen how the poor Pakistanis clung to the cloth of the Ka'bah; it was a sight for sore eyes.' I sobbed and only remember choking in a single expression: 'humiliated in Your presence'. For once, I was happy to be a 'poor Pakistani'.

There were others, too, who sobbed, but this was one time when a person wrapped up in him or herself didn't make a nasty little bundle; I was at His door. I wept bitterly, for my past, present and future,

I wept for what I believed was an existence in mud and actually hoped that someone would come from inside the door. For a Muslim, there is no physical point, 'defiled' as he or she may be, beyond that door and there I had reached. The burden of that moment was shattering.

As if that wasn't enough ... The silence that greeted me was deafening in its loudness. There was no glimmer of the emergence of a new being after being consumed by the flame. I sat there, drained and frightened, after what appeared to be hours of choking in 'humiliated in Your presence'. With my emptiness and nothingness complete, I stumbled away, repeating to myself: 'What did He have in mind to subject me to this apparently divine indifference?'

Much later, a body returned to complete the obligatory two *raka'at* (prayer units) at the Maqam al-Mahmud, the place where Abraham (Peace be upon him) is said to have prayed (Q. 2:125). A body went to drink from the sacred Zam Zam well, a body went to run between the hills of Saffa and Marwah in imitation of Hagar (Peace be upon her), the Black wife of Abraham, a body went to the hotel, a body returned to the *haram* five times a day for three days and a body got on to a bus which dropped it at the foot of the Mount of Light.

It was on this mountain that the Prophet Muhammad's anguished heart found solace through revelation, after being shattered. And who knows? I can always take a try. Anyway, I had nothing to lose. Being in the heat of summer, and at midday at that, there were no other bodies or souls around. Seven-year-old Musa looked at me quizzically for a few seconds before venturing to ask: 'Are you sure you don't want to wait till it is cooler?' 'Musa! Unlike your namesake in the Qur'an, I am not looking for a match or wood or fire. There is no flock awaiting me. I am alone and this journey is a matter of life and death for me. I want the mountain to be abandoned when I make my discovery. Musa, surely you understand all about these mountain trips?' The poor kid looked at me as if I was potty. (Not that he was very far off the mark, mind you.) I paid him for my bottle of spring water and started the ascent to the Cave of Hira'.

The Saudi regime, being very 'puritanical' and vehemently opposed to any form of 'unorthodox' veneration, does not encourage visits to any of the traditional sacred places. There are, thus, no official signs showing the path to the Cave of Hirah. You've got to follow the people. And if there are none around? Follow the Pepsi cans! Thousands and thousands of them, all along the route right up to the mouth of the cave, a few even littering its interior. What a sad spectacle! Along comes this 'follower' of Muhammad, his soul tied to Cook's American Dollar travellers' cheques, following a Pepsi-littered path and he says he is searching for Truth! Why don't you try another one, 'follower' of Muhammad?

Let me not be unfair to attempts by Muslims to outline the path for themselves. There were a few shoddily painted arrows pointing in the same direction as the Pepsi cans. Whatever little use these attempts to 'outline the path' may have been, was neutralized by the fact that there, in the same paint, in the same shoddy manner, were arrows pointing to exactly opposite directions! As if my agony at having to exorcize a thousand devils was not enough! As if having sheets of plastic ripped off the heads of our people at five o'clock on a cold winter morning in apartheid South Africa was not enough! As if having to mix sand with flour and feeding our children with it was not enough! As if two billion people going to bed on the floor or straw or dust at night, on empty stomachs, was not enough! As if ... And now, arrows pointing in opposite directions!

I continued following the Pepsi cans.

The path was steep and the journey agonizing. Along the way I noticed another guy with a Palestine scarf next to him, fast asleep. He, too, I said to myself, is a searcher. Let him also be. ('Also be'? And since when did it dawn upon you to be?) I eventually reached the cave, where I offered a lame two prayer units and studied the graffiti; the many 'Galiema and Fatima was here – 1967' and the numerous public declarations of love. I chuckled at the banality of it all and felt that perhaps there was nothing more to life than this.

So I have arrived and, well, if this is 'it' then so be it. Why not call it quits? The one side of the Mount of Light is rather steep and I looked down contemplating the time duration of my 'calling it quits'. In those few seconds my existence flashed in front of me. Just before doing what I wanted to do, I heard the voice of my fellow searcher, whom I thought I had long since left behind. *'Bhai jan! Ap ki; taswir khenchi? Sirf bis riyal hai?'* (My brother, can I take your photo? It will cost you only twenty riyals) – as he smilingly uncovered his Kodak Instamatic from the Palestinian scarf. He was in search of suckers.

I died my second death in as many days.

Some Sufis refer to 'the night of the spirit'. This was the culmination of my darkest night. I had been desperate to make sense of Islam and my relationship with Allah and now, for the first time, everything seemed so perfectly pointless. Upon my return to South Africa a curious even if seemingly unremarkable thing happened. The extent of my spiritual crisis was so severe that I simply had to reach out to others, even if only to ensure my physical survival. I met on a regular basis with three other close friends, Adli, Shamil and Ebrahim, to discuss the question of our own spiritual emptiness and struggles to lead lives of submission to the will of Allah in a racially divided and economically exploited society. From that support and discussion group grew the Call of Islam, a movement that was to play a very significant role in ensuring that Muslims were an integral, even if often unwilling, part of the struggle for non-racialism and non-sexism in South Africa. For a number of years I found this movement and, more specifically, the founding group, deeply supportive in my wrestling with Allah and self. Through them I developed a new appreciation of the verse in the Qur'an: 'Those who struggle in Us [Our path], unto them We shall show them Our ways' (Q. 29:69).

And so it appears as if Allah does have ideas for us, but that He does not panic when we do ... and that His ways are often so roundabout as to drive one around the bend ... and sometimes nearly over the cliff.

Source: Farid Esack, On Being a Muslim: Finding a Religious Path in the World Today *(Oxford: Oneworld, 1999), 12–17.*

EXERCISE

What information about the *hajj* does Esack provide, and what do you make of his account?

DISCUSSION

The article refers to some of the customs and rituals associated with *hajj*, including wearing the *ihram* (a simple two-piece cotton garment that all pilgrims wear) and rituals such as circumambulating the Ka'ba, running between the hills of Safa and Marwa in imitation of Hagar (Ibrahim/Abraham's wife), and drinking from the well at Zam Zam. It also refers to some unofficial practices, discouraged by the 'puritanical' Saudi authorities, such as scaling the side of Mount Hira to the spot where Muhammad received his early revelations. But most of all it provides a subjective reading of the experience, reminding us that Muslims approach *hajj* with all kinds of different experiences and concerns. It also introduces Islamic spirituality, especially important in the Sufi tradition, which reflects on inward experience. Thus Esack includes references to the philosopher and poet Muhammad Iqbal (1877–1938) and to the poet and mystic Jalal al-Din Rumi (1207–1273).

Esack also explains the sense in which Muslims experience *hajj* as a return to roots, both historically to the place where Muhammad received the first revelations, and personally: stripped of their diverse cultural identities and signs of material wealth, they work through the rituals together. Esack describes the experience of personal self-emptying bordering on a kind of breakdown: 'The poor kid looked at me as if I was potty. (Not that he was very far off the mark, mind you.)' But sharing his experience of struggle with his Muslims friends led eventually to the formation of a group that was to play an important role in ensuring Muslim participation in the anti-apartheid struggle in South Africa. □

The impact of *hajj*: wall paintings in Egypt

In Egypt there is a tradition of pilgrims painting the outside of their houses on their return from *hajj*. Two examples of this are shown in Plates 1 and 2 in the Visual Sources in this study guide.

EXERCISE

Look carefully at Plates 1 and 2. What do these wall paintings suggest about the contemporary experience and status of the *hajj*? What do you find most striking or interesting about them?

DISCUSSION

Visual records like these suggest that the experience of *hajj* remains a very important one for Muslims: in spite of the changes in means of travel and the increasing numbers of pilgrims, going on *hajj* remains a central religious experience which *hajjis* and *hajjas* want to celebrate publicly. Also, in addition to any information that they give about the experience of pilgrimage, one significant point to note about these images is that they illustrate the importance of visual representation in Islam. (We shall examine this in more detail later.) Thus, although there have been restrictions on visual representations of God, and this has even been extended to human figures and animals in some strict traditions, these paintings show how important visual images can be in popular culture in Muslim societies, including as an expression of piety.

This folk art draws on various styles and periods of both Islamic and non-Islamic art. In Plate 1, the pilgrim carrying an umbrella (to keep the sun off) is represented in a manner typical of ancient Egyptian images, whereas the adjacent figure on the prayer mat looks more like medieval Muslim representations of scholars. Combined with the detailed portrayal of a modern passenger jet soaring above both, the ensemble perhaps suggests the eternal unchanging nature of Allah and Islam throughout time, continuity and change in the experience of *hajj*, and the broad visual repertory of the painter.

Plate 2 shows both a wall painting and the woman whose experience is recorded in it. The representation of white-clad pilgrims surrounding the Ka'ba is reminiscent of the photograph in Figure 2 at the beginning of this section. The scene may underline the great visual and experiential impact this has on many people, as well as recording the focus of the pilgrimage. Here we see the contrast between the woman's black clothing in everyday life and her white robes when on *hajj*. □

Clearly the significance and impact of the *hajj* on individuals is varied; it may be affected by gender, nationality, expectations and personal experience. For some it is life changing, and for many it confirms a great sense of participating in a truly global community of believers. By looking at the impact of the *hajj* experience on various individuals we realise that Islam is a vibrant, lived reality for people from a wide variety of cultural and geographical backgrounds.

Other forms of pilgrimage

Although, as one of the Five Pillars, the *hajj* is the most central and best-known form of pilgrimage associated with Islam, it should be noted that there are other pilgrimage destinations and foci. As we shall see later, some Sufis travel to the shrines of holy men, while for Shi'ite Muslims, going on pilgrimage to Karbala has a similar significance to going on *hajj* to Mecca. After the fall of Saddam Hussein in 2003, it became possible for Iraqi Muslims to make pilgrimages outside Iraq (in spite of the security dangers in 2004) for the first time in more than thirty years. You can see scenes from the 2004 pilgrimage on the DVD, which you will be directed to watch when we consider Ruthven, Chapter 3, and after you have been introduced to the events which it commemorates in the early history of Shi'ism.

3
Leadership and law

Begin your work in this section by reading Ruthven, 'Institutional leadership' and 'Legal modernization', on pages 14 to 17.

EXERCISE

1 Who are the *'ulama*?

2 How has their role developed over the centuries?

3 In what ways have Muslims responded to the challenges posed by modernity to Muslim legal traditions?

DISCUSSION

1 The *'ulama,* literally translatable as 'learned men', are scholars trained in the interpretation of Islamic tradition, including its legal aspects. In the absence of a centralised religious authority equivalent to the papacy in Western Christianity, the *'ulama* provide a kind of diffused counterbalance to the authority of political leaders. Some *'ulama* are chosen by political leaders to become their *mufti*, someone respected as an interpreter of the law, and who therefore issues legal judgements (*fatawa*: singular *fatwa*) on a variety of issues. Other *'ulama* become judges (*qadis*) in religious (*shari'a*) courts.

2 The extent of the jurisdiction of *shari'a* courts has varied, with caliphal courts often dealing with criminal matters in Islamic empires such as the Ottoman Empire, restricting the powers of the *shari'a* courts to family and business matters. Under colonial rule, this pattern often persisted, with Western law increasingly adopted in criminal courts. The *'ulama* have lost prestige in the modern period, as secular educated Muslims have often taken control of political and legal systems, although in societies with fewer modernising influences the *'ulama* have sometimes tried to take power directly. In the first case, argues Ruthven, the subtleties of the Islamic legal tradition are neglected in a crude attempt to 'Islamize' societies. In the second case, the complexities of modern life are ignored. In both cases, an effective legal hermeneutics (interpretation) fails, because this would require a strong grasp of both the legal tradition and modern life.

3 Some Muslims have attempted to reconcile Islamic and Western legal codes. Radical Muslims call for a 'restoration' of *shari'a*, which in practice often involves a focus on punishments and aspects of the

criminal law which are symbolic of Islamic resistance to the 'decadent' West, such as flogging for sexual offences. Others have focused on trying to find ways of financial risk-sharing that do not rely on payment of interest. Ruthven's view, however, is that calls to restore *shari'a* are often based more on an uncritical idealisation of the past and overdrawn contrasts with other societies. □

The Islamic state, Islamic civilisation, and Muslim ideas of a 'Golden Age'

What is an 'Islamic state'? Muslims who see Islam as a political ideology tend to describe one of their aims as the creation of an 'Islamic state'. An important part of what they mean by this is the 'implementation of *shari'a*' (Islamic law). However, critics argue that this proposal, which may at first seem straightforward (whether one agrees with it or not), is actually highly problematic. Two main reasons are given for this. First, Muslim societies have historically tended to be legally plural – that is, not just governed by *shari'a*. Secondly, *shari'a* is not simply a set of rules that can be straightforwardly implemented, but rather the outcome of a careful process of interpreting Islamic sources in response to changing conditions. On pages 17 to 21, Ruthven examines the historical experiences that underlie Muslim appeals to an earlier 'golden age', and introduces some of the achievements and features of Islamic civilisation. Read this section, 'Successes and failures of the Islamic state', now.

EXERCISE

1 What kinds of cultural achievements are associated with Islamic civilisation, and during what period did these occur?

2 What does 'Islamicate' mean and why was the term introduced?

3 How did the relationship between the Arab tribal leaders and the *'ulama* develop?

4 Why did kinship remain a more important element in the organisation of Muslim societies than in Europe, and what long-term consequences has this had?

DISCUSSION

1 Ruthven mentions 'architecture and design, metalwork and ceramics, poetry and philosophy, [and] ... "harder" sciences including mathematics, optics, astronomy, and medicine' (2012, 17). He says that these achievements occurred 'several centuries before the Renaissance in Europe', that is, in the tenth to twelfth centuries CE.

2 'Islamicate' is a term introduced by the American historian Marshall Hodgson to describe societies in which Islam is the dominant religious tradition, but other cultural elements and religious traditions are also present. Although Ruthven states that the term 'probably raises as many questions as it answers', it is a useful shorthand way of indicating that few Muslim-majority societies have ever been entirely Muslim, but have usually included Christian, Jewish and other elements. It also indicates the important influence of Islam on the culture and institutions of such societies.

3 After his death, Muhammad was succeeded by four caliphs (literally 'deputies'), known in Sunni tradition as the 'Rightly Guided' caliphs, who were elected by popular acclamation among the elders of the community. After the death of the last of these ('Ali, who was caliph from 656–661 CE), disputes developed over the religious and political leadership of the Muslim community. Among the group who came to be the majority – the Sunnis – political authority was assumed by the Umayyad dynasty, and the role of caliph became hereditary, whereas religious knowledge became the province of the '*ulama*. It was in this context that the division between military rulers, who were often Bedouin tribal leaders or their descendants, and the religious authority of the '*ulama* developed. One later caliph – al-Mamun in the ninth century – tried to reassert caliphal religious authority, but failed, and this consolidated the office of the '*ulama* as guardians of Islamic orthodoxy. As we shall see in more detail in Ruthven, Chapter 3, after the death of 'Ali, the roles of political and religious leadership remained more closely intertwined in the minority Shi'ite tradition, and it was believed that leadership of the Islamic community should remain in the Prophet's bloodline, a claim that was not made either by the Umayyads or their successors in the Sunni caliphate.

4 On page 20 Ruthven argues that the lack of a central institution (equivalent to the Christian Church in medieval Europe) independent of kinship and tribal loyalties created difficulties for the development of strong institutions in Islamicate societies. On page 21 he argues that this had long-term implications for political development: a 'civil society', independent of both the state and kinship ties, did not develop, and the institutions of the state did not penetrate deeply into society, but rather 'sat on top of' it. □

The spread of Islam and Islamic civilisation

After the death of Muhammad (632 CE), the expansion of the Islamic empire continued rapidly. As you can see from the map of 'Muslims in the World' in Ruthven, page xv, by 644 it extended from North Africa in the West (present-day Tunisia) to central Asia (present-day Afghanistan) in the east. By 750 it had expanded west right across North Africa and into the Iberian peninsula (contemporary Spain and Portugal), and as far east as Sind (part of Pakistan today).

Arguably this period of rapid expansion had long-term political consequences, for the classical legal texts of the period all assume eventual Islamic political leadership. Although this early expansion was led by military conquest, the Arab armies did not uniformly enforce the conversion of conquered peoples, whose conversion followed gradually, if at all. Later, in the medieval period, Islam was to spread to South-East Asia and sub-Saharan Africa primarily through trade.

The nature of Islamic revival

Now read Ruthven, 'A religious awakening?' and 'Or a spiritual vacuum?' on pages 21 to 23.

EXERCISE

1 What are the signs of Islamic resurgence, and what reasons have been suggested for this resurgence?

2 How has Sufism been important in Muslim history, and what has been the relationship between Sufism and Islamic resurgence?

DISCUSSION

1 Ruthven has already discussed the political mobilisation of Islam, and this is perhaps the most prominent way that Islam is portrayed in the media – but it is a use of Islam over which Muslims disagree. There has, however, also been a more everyday and 'spiritual' side too. These are what Ruthven introduces here. Signs of revival in everyday life include increased mosque attendance and fasting, a growth in religious publications in various forms, and adoption of 'Islamic dress', especially by women. He discusses two possible reasons for these developments. First, rapid urbanisation can lead to a breakdown of traditional social structures, and exposure (especially through the media) to Western customs, which may be perceived as alien and threatening. In response, people may turn to religious traditions in the new forms in which they become available in urban life – in mosque-based associations and groups. Secondly, these mosque-based networks become particularly important both practically and politically in societies where the state fails to meet people's material needs, and where sources of direct political opposition are repressed. Ruthven also mentions a further factor in urban environments – the role of information technology in

undercutting the religious authority of the *'ulama*, by making alternative interpretations of sacred sources more widely available.

2 Sufism has been very important for the transmission of Islamic tradition in Muslim history. Whereas the *'ulama* have provided continuity to Islam's outward practices, the Sufi orders have been vehicles for mediating the inward and spiritual experience of *iman* (faith). However, Ruthven suggests that the experience of modernisation has been a difficult one for these groups, especially the suppression of Sufi groups by nationalist governments stamping down on any possible source of opposition – for example, in Turkey. Some scholars – such as Peter von Sivers – have also linked the decline of Sufism with the rise of Islamic political movements. We shall examine Sufism further in our discussion of Ruthven, Chapter 4. □

Revival across the Muslim world? The results of a survey

The next reading comes from a study led by Riaz Hassan that surveyed the opinions of Muslims in four different Muslim-majority societies (Egypt, Indonesia, Pakistan and Kazakhstan) in the late 1990s. The first three of these societies are the largest Muslim-majority societies in the world, and Kazakhstan is a good example of a post-communist society with a large number of Muslims. The study asked respondents a series of questions on their understanding of Islam and its relationship to different aspects of contemporary life: gender, work, social attitudes and politics. The term 'respondent' here refers to someone who answered the survey. *Pirs/Kiyai* are traditional Sufi leaders.

READING 3

Muslim piety

The ritualistic dimension – religious practice

Islam is a ritual-rich religion, and Muslims are required to perform specific rituals as a religious duty or as an expression of their faith. Four religious rituals commonly performed by Muslims were used to ascertain the ritual dimension in this study: performance of daily prayers; payment of Zakat; fasting in the month of Ramadan; and the recitation of the Holy Qur'an. The results of the investigation are reported in the following section.

Performance of daily prayers

All adult Muslims are required to observe prayers five times a day as a religious duty. Respondents were asked, 'How often do your perform

Salat?' They were offered a number of responses which are listed in Table 2.8. Indonesian respondents observed their duty to pray most strictly, with 96 per cent of them praying five times or more daily. They were followed by the Egyptians, of whom 90 per cent prayed five or more times every day. Only 57 per cent of Pakistanis prayed five times or more. The Kazakhs were the least observant of the daily prayers, with only five per cent indicating that they prayed more than five times a day. In fact, an overwhelming percentage of Kazakhs either never prayed or only prayed sometimes. The evidence, therefore, reveals significant diversity in observing mandatory daily prayers among Muslims.

Table 2.8 Perform Salat

	Indonesia	**Pakistan**	**Kazakhstan**	**Egypt**
Number	1472	1185	1000	786
One to four times daily	1.4%	19%	3.7%	3.1%
Five times a day	47	46	4	70
More than five times a day	49	11	0.8	20
Only on Fridays	0.1	5	2	–
Only on special occasions	0.4	3	9	1
Never	0.1	10	67	3
Occasionally/Sometimes	2	5	14	2

Payment of Zakat and fasting

Two other practices expected of a Muslim are the payment of *Zakat* (poor tax) and a fasting in the month of Ramadan. Respondents were asked if they had paid Zakat and fasted during the previous twelve months. The results reported in Table 2.9a show that for Zakat the pattern was similar to the one observed in the case of prayers. Indonesians and Egyptians were significantly stricter observants of their Zakat duty than Pakistanis and Kazakhs. In relation to fasting, Indonesians, Egyptians and Pakistanis reported almost universal observance, whereas only 19 per cent of the Kazakhs reported having fasted during the past year (Table 2.9b).

Table 2.9a Paid Zakat

	Indonesia	**Pakistan**	**Kazakhstan**	**Egypt**
Number	1472	1185	1000	786
Yes	94%	58%	49%	87%
No	6	39	50	13

Note: Figures exclude 'no response'.

Table 2.9b Fasted

	Indonesia	**Pakistan**	**Kazakhstan**	**Egypt**
Number	1472	1185	1000	786
Yes	99%	93%	19%	99%
No	1	5	81	1

Note: Figures exclude 'no response'.

[...]

In Islam, many Muslims pray privately, which is beyond their formal religious duties. One act of devotion which is both private and spontaneous for Muslims is their commitment to the Holy Qur'an, and belief that its teaching is the best guide to behaviour. Consequently, many Muslims consult the Qur'an for guidance in their daily lives.

In this study the respondents were asked, 'Thinking now of your daily life and the decisions you have to make about how to spend your time, how to act with other people, how to bring up your children, presuming you have them, and so on, to what extent does what you have read in the Qur'an help you in making everyday decisions?' The respondents were given a number of options and asked to indicate the one that applied to them most closely.

The responses, as well as the distribution of respondents in the four countries, are given in Table 2.12. The findings show that if we combine the two response categories, 'I can remember specific times when it has helped me in a very direct way in making decisions' and 'I often consult the Qur'an to make specific decisions', then the Indonesians are the most devoted, followed by the Egyptians and Pakistanis. The Kazakhs once again are the least devoted. This finding is consistent with the findings reported above about ritualism.

Table 2.12 How the Qur'an helps you in making everyday decisions

	Indonesia	Pakistan	Kazakhstan	Egypt
Number	1472	1170	1000	786
I hardly think of the Qur'an as I go about my daily life	2%	33%	45%	13%
I can't think of specific examples, nevertheless I feel sure that the Qur'an is still of help in my daily life	34	17	20	33
I can remember specific times when it has helped me in a very direct way in making decisions	23	44	11	16
I often consult the Qur'an to make specific decisions	41	5	5	36
Other	1	1	19	2

[...]

The Consequential Dimension

The consequential dimension refers to the secular effect of religious belief, practice and experience. Religious beliefs and ideologies invariably compete with other beliefs and ideologies (i.e., magic, science) in society as explanations of questions dealing with the meanings and nature of the ultimate divine reality and the nature and purposes of human life, condition and destiny. In modern times science has become the major rival of religion in explaining the nature, purposes and meanings of human conditions and destiny. The beliefs and statements which counter some core religious beliefs usually evoke social and psychological pressures on the individual to reject such beliefs.

In this study two questions were used to investigate the consequential religiosity. The questions were 'Do you agree that a person who says there is no Allah is likely to hold dangerous political views?' and 'Do you agree or disagree with Darwin's theory of evolution?' These questions were chosen because they challenged two fundamental religious beliefs widely held by Muslims. For each question the respondents were offered multiple choice type responses which are indicated in Tables 2.15a and 2.15b.

Table 2.15a Would you agree that a person who says there is no Allah is likely to hold dangerous and political views?

	Indonesia	**Pakistan**	**Kazakhstan**	**Egypt**
Number	1472	1167	1000	783
Agree	84%	74%	19%	89%
Disagree	7	14	50	11
Uncertain	9	12	31	0.1

Table 2.15b Do you agree or disagree with Darwin's theory of evolution?

	Indonesia	**Pakistan**	**Kazakhstan**	**Egypt**
Number	1472	1173	1000	785
The theory is almost certainly true	2%	5%	10%	3%
The theory is probably true	14	9	27	5
The theory is probably false	11	12	14	15
The theory could not possibly be true	61	60	14	52
I never thought about this before	12	14	35	25

The findings show that, with the exception of Kazakhstan, an overwhelming majority of people in Indonesia, Pakistan and Egypt agreed that a person who does not believe in Allah is likely to hold dangerous views. In Kazakhstan a majority of persons did not think so, or were uncertain about the consequences of disbelief in Allah. Similarly, Darwin's theory of evolution was held to be false by a majority of the respondents in Indonesia, Pakistan and Egypt. In Kazakhstan two or three times the respondents in the other three countries expressed qualified or unqualified support of the theory, and one-third of the Kazakh respondents said that they had never thought about the theory.

[...]

The respondents in all four countries were asked how much trust they had in key institutions of the state and civil society. The analysis in this chapter is based on the response to that question which was posed as follows: 'I am going to name a number of organizations. For each one, could you tell me how much you trust them to tell the truth and to do what is best for the country? It is, a great deal of trust, quite a lot of trust, not very much trust, none at all, or do not know?' The institutions about which the respondents' opinions were sought were the following:

Ulama	Parliament	Press	Universities
Imam Masjid	Courts	Television	Schools
Pirs/Kiyai	Civil Service	Major Companies	Intellectuals
	Political Parties		
	Armed Forces		

In computing the trust scores from the data the two categories of 'a great deal of trust' and 'quite a lot of trust' were combined to arrive at a composite index of trust. Similarly, the 'do not trust' categories were combined, and the single score for this was generated by combining the two low trust categories with the 'do not know' category.

The findings of the survey data are reported in Table 5.1 They show that there are wide variations as well as similarities among respondents in the four countries in terms of their trust in core institutions of religion and the state. Kazakhstan stands out as a country in which Muslims universally have very low confidence in the key institutions of society. This is most likely a function of the dramatic changes that have occurred in Kazakhstan over the past decade. The impression gathered during the fieldwork was that most people were disoriented by the economic and social changes that followed the collapse of the former Soviet Union. These changes had reduced the total worth of Kazakhstan's Gross Domestic Product by half, thus adversely affecting the lives of ordinary citizens. Many of them were disillusioned and very apprehensive about the future, and the data reflect this. In relative terms, roughly three out of ten respondents trusted the armed forces, press, television, universities and intellectuals. However, the religious institutions of the ulama, Imam masjid and pirs enjoyed much more trust than the key institutions of the state. This is rather surprising, given that most Kazakhs were not actively involved in religion during the Soviet era. As argued earlier Kazakhstan would need to be considered a special case. The other three countries can be compared with greater confidence.

Table 5.1 Trust in Key Institutions (%)

Institution	**Pakistan**	**Indonesia**	**Egypt**	**Kazakhstan**
Ulama	48	96	90	24
Imam Masjid	44	94	83	22
Pirs/Kiyai	21	91	52	21
Parliament	22	53	34	19
Courts	55	55	76	16
Civil Service	26	58	44	11
Political Parties	12	35	28	12
Armed Forces	82	68	78	33
Press	38	84	54	33
Television	31	80	49	37
Major Companies	29	42	45	14
Universities	60	88	70	33
Schools	71	92	68	48
Intellectuals	66	92	81	37

Source: Riaz Hassan, Faithlines: Muslim Conceptions of Islam and Society *(Oxford: Oxford University Press, 2002), 54–5, 58, 64–5, 152–3.*

EXERCISE

1 What proportion of respondents in each of these societies claims to perform *salat* at least five times a day?

2 What proportion of respondents in each country claims that the Qur'an helps them to make everyday decisions?

3 What is the 'consequential' dimension of religiosity, and how do attitudes to the political views of atheists and Darwin's theory of evolution demonstrate this dimension?

4 To what extent does Table 5.1 in Reading 3 support Ruthven's argument that confidence in the *'ulama* is being eroded by new media for the transmission of religious traditions, or that Sufism is losing ground to political Islam?

DISCUSSION

1 The proportion that claims to perform *salat* five times a day or more is: 96 per cent in Indonesia (47% + 49%), 57 per cent in Pakistan (46% + 11%), 4.8 per cent in Kazakhstan (4% + 0.8%), and 90 per cent in Egypt (70% + 20%). Caution needs to be exercised in interpreting these results as a reflection of actual practice – respondents may wish to reflect a favourable impression of their piety to an investigator!

2 The proportion that claims that the Qur'an helps them to make everyday decisions is: 98 per cent in Indonesia, (34 + 23 + 41), 66 per cent in Pakistan (17 + 44 + 5), 36 per cent in Kazakhstan (20 +11 + 5), and 85 per cent in Egypt (33 + 16 + 36). Note that this result conflates several responses – those unable to think of specific examples with those who can, and those who claim that they often consult the Qur'an for advice. As well as the gap between practice and what people say they do, it is also important to note that how questions are worded can make a big difference to the response.

3 The consequential dimension means the difference belief makes to everyday life – in this case to attitudes to political authority and scientific theory. Small majorities (between 52 and 61 per cent) in the three more observant societies reject Darwinism out of hand – presumably because it is believed to conflict with Qur'anic revelation; beyond these majorities, between 11 and 15 per cent are highly sceptical – considering the theory 'probably false'. The issue of how a question is interpreted by respondents may be particularly important when considering these responses on Darwinism – the term may have been interpreted in a variety of ways. The study also shows that large majorities in the more religiously observant societies consider that atheists are likely to hold dangerous political views. This suggests that religion and politics are seen as intimately linked by many in these societies.

4 Table 5.1 offers little support for Ruthven's contention that the authority of the *'ulama* has been much undermined: the *'ulama* are the most trusted institution in each of the more religiously observant societies, with ratings of over 90 per cent in Egypt and Indonesia. However, the argument that Sufism is losing ground to political Islam may receive some support, because confidence in *pirs/kiyai* is considerably lower than that of the *'ulama* in Pakistan and Egypt,

both countries with active Islamist movements – though so too has Indonesia, where confidence remains high. ☐

Islam and Islamism

Now read Ruthven, 'Conclusion: Islam and Islamism', pages 23 to 26.

EXERCISE

How does Ruthven describe the process of Islamic religious revival?

DISCUSSION

Ruthven states that social and technological change, especially the disruption caused by rapid urbanisation, is linked to Islamic revival, and he compares this with the increased activity of Protestant churches in similar contexts in Latin America and sub-Saharan Africa. However, for Islam, revival in religious practice is linked to politics, because of problems with governments in many Muslim-majority societies. Next, Ruthven argues that the authority of the main historic bearers of religious tradition in Islam – the '*ulama* and Sufi brotherhoods – has been challenged by a range of movements and leaders. This process has been facilitated by mass literacy and new media technologies, which have made Islamic sources available to wider publics. The pattern of religious revival movements challenging traditional authorities, and sometimes seizing political power, has occurred before in Muslim history. However, modern political revivalist movements are distinctive partly because of the technology they mobilise, and partly because they import ideas from outside the Muslim intellectual tradition, although they are selective in what they use from it.

Ruthven argues that 'Islamism' is a better word than 'fundamentalism' to describe these groups because, as with the development of the ideology of 'communism' from 'commune', these groups take a pre-existing entity – in this case Islamic religion – and redefine its content. ☐

Alternative views on the social bases of Islamism

It is important to note that Islamic revival and politics is a complex topic, and that different scholars, journalists and politicians, among others, have developed (and continue to develop) different theories to try to understand it. For example, the work of the American anthropologist Gregory Starrett (1998) provides a rather different perspective from that of Ruthven. Starrett's theory was developed from fieldwork conducted in the suburbs of Cairo in the early to mid-1990s. He identifies many of the same processes at work as Ruthven – urbanisation, increases in literacy, the use of new technology to transmit Islamic traditions, political oppression and the government's problems in meeting the material needs and desires of the people. But he draws slightly different conclusions. First, he is sceptical about the central role given to dislocation caused by urbanisation in Ruthven's account. He argues that in Egypt the main factor that has undermined the prestige of traditional religious education (and hence of traditional educators – the '*ulama*) has been the growth of state education, and this factor is present in both rural and urban areas.

Secondly, Starrett questions the fit between political ideology and social group suggested by Ruthven. This is because he finds little evidence that those who have been most affected by rural–urban migration – the urban poor – are most inclined to join Islamist movements. Rather, the composition of Islamist groups is similar to that of other political associations: that is, the better educated predominate. This leads him to interpret the explosion of Islamic publishing (including print, audio and web-based communication) rather differently from Ruthven. Instead of confused and bewildered rural migrants falling victim to 'demagogues', he sees well-educated Muslims, influenced by a state education that has taught them to see Islam as a practical resource, reading Islamic sacred sources for themselves and seeking answers to contemporary problems. Thus, whereas Ruthven tends to see ordinary followers frustrated by hardship and misled by power-hungry leaders, Starrett sees people empowered by education using the tools that education has put at their disposal to challenge the political status quo.

We may conclude from this that the Islamic political revival is a complex phenomenon and scholars disagree over how to explain it. In fact Ruthven does also mention the impact of mass education, and both he and Starrett agree that educational developments have played a major role in undermining the authority of the traditional religious leaders. They agree that this has opened up a gap which has been filled by new movements and leaders, 'most of whom claim a religious legitimacy for their acts' (2012, 25). In Egypt the most important of these, it is worth pointing out here, continues to be the Muslim Brotherhood; Ruthven discusses this movement on pages 138–9.

There is also evidence that some individuals are heavily influenced by charismatic preachers – there are some examples of this in the UK too, and in the commentary on Ruthven, Chapter 6, we will consider the case of Zacarias Moussaoui, who allegedly had planned to be one of the hijackers in the attack on New York and Washington on September 11th, 2001, and whose upbringing and influences are described by his brother in Reading 12.

However, the dismissal of the Islamic Trend as simply ideology, and the mass of its followers as led astray by demagogues, does not do justice to the complexity, depth or scope of this movement, nor to the quest for social justice that many influenced by it believe they are engaged in. In part, the rights and wrongs of Islamism need to be judged against what is actually said in Islam's sacred sources, and in discussing Ruthven's Chapter 2 we shall turn to this.

But before we do, we shall examine another brief passage from Farid Esack, whose experiences of *hajj* we discussed earlier. Esack is critical of extremist forms of Islam, but also keen to build on the desire for justice he discerns within Islamic revival movements. After this, I shall ask you to complete a brief reflective exercise.

READING 4

What's the bottom line in this book?

There is an exciting and challenging wind of relevance blowing through the world of Islam. Numerous Muslims, especially among the young, are keen to know how Islam relates to our here and now. Many responses have been forthcoming as a part of this wind of relevance: these are often vague, repetitive, superficial and, at times, even alarming. Some of these responses are alarming not only to those who desire to be unfettered in their march to entrench their control over the global economy but also to many Muslims who value social justice and personal freedom. Alhamdulillah (Praise be to Allah), of the latter breed there is a growing band.

The more strident, angry and fanatical displays of this revival receive a great deal of attention. This should not, however, detract from the genuineness of the 'new Muslim'. This Muslim is new in the sense that she is adamant that a stagnant and fossilized Islam confined to a set of rituals that are mere motions must make way for a personally meaningful and socially relevant Islam. Those of us who are deeply committed to a human and compassionate expression of our faith cannot allow ourselves to be swamped by the noise of religious obscurantism and the equally destructive caricaturing in some sections of the media of the whole of Islam as a threat to civilized values.

Much of the emphasis in contemporary works on Islam by committed Muslims has hitherto been on the more obviously ideological aspects of Islam. These works usually cater for those who simply see Islam as an alternative to the universal colonization of consciousness through a process of relentless McDonaldization, the accompanying destruction of local cultures and economic exploitation. Two other factors have contributed to the sharp, rather angry and often dehumanizing image of Islam. These are the suffering endured by Muslims in several parts of the world such as in Palestine, Chechnya, the Balkans and Kashmir, and a simplistic recourse to our religious heritage as both our safe haven and the mother of all weapons.

I believe that there is a path between dehumanizing fundamentalism and fossilized traditionalism. This is a path of radical Islam committed to social justice, to individual liberty and the quest for the Transcendent who is beyond all institutional religious and dogmatic constructions; an Islam that challenges us to examine our faith in personally and socially relevant terms. This Islam, I believe, provides a set of personal responses in an increasingly materialistic society where most people are living, and very many dying, lives of quiet desperation with a frightening sense of alienation from themselves, others and Allah. Muslims *can* make an effective contribution alongside those of other religious convictions to the creation of a world wherein it is safe to be human.

One of the things that often distinguishes religious groups from other ideological groups is our commitment to personal introspection. We struggle not only to examine the socio-economic structures that create and entrench oppression but also examine our personal roles in, as well as reactions to, them. We ask questions such as 'How do we relate to our faith in concrete terms?', 'How do we become "witness bearers for Allah" in an unjust society?', 'How do we strengthen ourselves in a common commitment to establish a just order on earth?' and 'How do we commit ourselves to others in an atmosphere of honesty and acceptance?' Our personal responses to these questions are, in the final analysis, the only barometer of our commitment to a holistic Islam.

It must, however, be emphasized that this re-examination or reviewing of our faith in personal terms cannot be done in isolation from the struggle to work against unjust socio-economic systems. Islam was never nurtured in a protective hothouse; the history of early Islam was a continuous struggle of socio-political engagement, introspection, revelation and more engagement.

Source: Farid Esack, On Being a Muslim: Finding a Religious Path in the World Today *(Oxford: Oneworld, 1999), 1–3.*

EXERCISE

1 What are the characteristics of the 'new Muslim'?

2 What, in Esack's view, often distinguishes religious groups from other ideological groups?

DISCUSSION

1 First of all, Esack, a male, uses the female pronoun to characterise the 'new Muslim'. Why has he done this? Perhaps it is a strategy to destabilise the assumption that 'the Muslim' stereotype is typically male, or perhaps to write against gender bias in Western as well as Muslim literature. This new Muslim seeks a 'personally meaningful' and 'socially relevant' Islam, a path between 'dehumanizing fundamentalism' and 'religious obscurantism' that is committed to 'social justice', 'individual liberty' and 'the quest for the Transcendent'. It can provide part of an alternative to a 'materialistic society'.

2 According to Esack, personal introspection distinguishes religious from other ideological groups. This seems to involve self-questioning as part of a faith whose source and goal is always transcendent, both within and beyond the individual and material world. In this passage, the 'new Muslim' is clearly an ideal, yet one struggling to come into being in the often difficult circumstances of contemporary Muslims. In the final sentence, Esack describes early Muslim history as a continual process of engagement, introspection and revelation, leading to further engagement, introspection, and so on. This was the pattern of the Prophet Muhammad's life, and it is a pattern that Muslims seek to follow. ☐

EXERCISE: A FINAL REFLECTION ON CHAPTER 1

Please return to the list of impressions or associations with Islam that you wrote down at the beginning of this section of the study guide. How many of these have you found referred to in the readings so far? Are there new characteristics you have come across that have made you look at things differently? ☐

4
The Qur'an and the Prophet

Begin this section by reading Ruthven, Chapter 2, pages 27 to 28 as far as 'The Quran'.

EXERCISE

1 Why were Muslims called 'Muhammadans' in the early twentieth century, and why is this title no longer used?

2 What is the distinction between the two kinds of Muhammad's utterances?

DISCUSSION

1 Muslims were mistakenly called 'Muhammadans' because the importance of Muhammad to Muslims was mistaken by Europeans for worship, just as Christians worship Jesus. But although Muhammad's words and actions are very important for Muslims, Muhammad himself is not regarded as divine, as Christ is for traditional Christians. Rather, the absolute distinction between Allah and creation, including humanity, is central to Islam. Hence the term 'Muslim', 'one who submits [to the will of God]' is the best term for followers of Islam.

2 Muslims distinguish between the words of Muhammad when directly inspired by God, which are recorded in the Qur'an (literally, 'recitation'), and words spoken in his normal human capacity, which are recorded in the *hadith* ('tradition') literature. The latter are regarded as authoritative guidance for Muslims, but not as the direct words of God. ☐

Now read Ruthven, 'The Quran', pages 28 to 36, including the text in boxes.

EXERCISE

1 How do Muslims regard the words of the Qur'an, and how is this status reflected in the rituals surrounding its use?

2 How was the Qur'an revealed and recorded?

3 What is the Fatiha? What is its significance, and how has it been incorporated into Islamic ritual?

4 How is the text of the Qur'an organised, and what kind of material does it contain?

DISCUSSION

1 Most Muslims regard the Qur'an as the 'speech of God, dictated without human editing'. Indeed, it came to be regarded as 'uncreated', not made by God but with God from the beginning of time – like the person of Christ in traditional Christianity. This exalted status is reflected in several rituals. First, Muslims must ritually wash themselves before handling the text of the Qur'an. Secondly, when it is recited, set words are said before and after it. Thirdly, it is believed that some of the verses have special properties: for example, the first chapter is recited to combat scorpion bites.

2 The revelations are believed to have been received by Muhammad between 610 and 632 CE. Muhammad went into a trance-like state while he received the revelations, and some were written down during his lifetime. After his death in 632 they were collected by his successors, the first four caliphs (deputies), with an official version agreed under the third caliph 'Uthman (644–656 CE). However, partly because the earliest Arabic lacked 'diacritical marks' – marks on the text to indicate which vowels are to be used between consonants in the middle of words – slightly different versions continued in use. These were eventually reduced to seven, regarded as equally valid.

3 The Fatiha is the opening surah ('row' or 'chapter') of the Qur'an. It proclaims the nature of God as merciful and compassionate, deserving of exclusive service and worship, lord of creation and master of the day of judgement, and thereby implying a belief in life after death and human accountability for our actions. Thus, according to Muhammad Asad, it 'contains all the fundamental principles laid down in the Qur'an'. It is incorporated into Muslim ritual by being recited during *salat*, which, as we have seen, is one of the Five Pillars of Islam.

4 The Qur'an is organised into 114 surahs, arranged in order of length from longest to shortest, except for the Fatiha. It contains stories about figures familiar to those acquainted with Jewish and Christian scriptures, such as Adam, Moses and Jesus (Isa), as well as some Arabian figures (Hud, Salih, Luqman). Each of these is presented as a prophet sent to warn people to follow righteousness and worship God alone. *Shirk* – association of God with anything else – is seen as an especially serious error. The Qur'an has no overall narrative structure (no story running through it), but material is grouped thematically. Muhammad is mentioned only four times. The style is often indirect and difficult to understand without contextual knowledge. This and the lack of narrative structure have been used as arguments for its

authenticity, since any editor would presumably have made it easier to understand by referring to context or developing plot. □

The contents of the Qur'an: a closer look

This section contains a long extract from John L. Esposito, *Islam: The Straight Path* (1988). The reading is interspersed with exercises for you to consider.

Muhammad and the Quran

READING 5

The Quran: the Word of God

For Muslims, the Quran is the Book of God. It is the eternal, uncreated, literal word of God sent down from heaven, revealed one final time to the Prophet Muhammad as a guide for humankind (2:185). The Quran consists of 114 chapters of 6,000 verses, originally revealed to Muhammad over a period of twenty-two years. It is approximately four-fifths the size of the New Testament, and its chapters are arranged according to length, not chronology. The longer chapters, representing the later Medinan revelations, precede the shorter, earlier Meccan revelations to Muhammad.

Islam teaches that God's revelation has occurred in several forms: in nature, history, and Scripture. God's existence can be known through creation; nature contains pointers or 'signs' of God, its creator and sustainer (3:26–27). The history of the rise and fall of nations, victory and defeat, provides clear signs and lessons of God's sovereignty and intervention in history (30:2–9). In addition, God in His mercy determined to reveal His will for humankind through a series of messengers: 'Indeed, We sent forth among every nation a Messenger, saying "Serve your God, and shun false gods"' (16:36) (see also 13:7, 15:10, 35:24). The verses of revelation are also called signs of God. Thus, throughout history, human beings could not only know that there is a God but also know what God desires and commands for His creatures.

If Scripture is a sign from God sent to previous generations, what can be said about these Scriptures and prophets? Why was the Quran subsequently revealed, and what is the relationship of the Quran and Muhammad to previous revelations?

Although God has revealed His will to Moses and the Hebrew prophets and later to Jesus, Muslims believe that the Scriptures of the Jewish community (Torah) and that of the Christian church (the Evangel or Gospel) were corrupted. The current texts of the

Torah and the New Testament are regarded as a composite of human fabrications mixed with divine revelation. Of God's revelation to the Jews, the Quran declares:

> Surely We sent down the Torah, wherein is guidance and light; thereby the Prophets who had surrendered themselves gave judgment for those of Jewry, as did the masters and rabbis, following that portion of God's book as they were given to keep and were witness to. (5:47)

Muslims believe that after the deaths of the prophets, extraneous, nonbiblical beliefs infiltrated the texts and thus altered and distorted the original, pure revelation. The Jews, and later the Christians, are portrayed as having distorted their mission to witness into a doctrine of their divine election as a chosen people:

> And the Jews and Christians say 'We are the sons of God, and His beloved ones.' Say: 'Why then does He chastise you for your sins? No you are the mortals, of His creating; He forgives whom He will, and He chastises whom He will.' (5:20)

The Quran teaches that a similar degeneration or perversion of Scripture occurred in Christianity. God sent Jesus as a prophet: 'He (God) will teach him [Jesus] the Book, the Wisdom, the Torah, the Gospel, to be a messenger to the Children of Israel' (3:48–49). Yet, the Quran declares that after his death Jesus' meaning and message were soon altered by those who made him into a god:

> The Christians say, 'The Messiah is the Son of God.'... God assail them! How they are perverted! ... They were commanded to serve but One God; There is no God but He. (9:30–31)

After the falsification of the revelation given to the Jews and the Christians, Muslims believe that God in His mercy sent down His word one final time. The Quran does not abrogate or nullify, but rather corrects, the versions of Scripture preserved by the Jewish and Christian communities: 'People of the Book, now there has come to you Our messenger making clear to you many things you have been concealing of the Book, and effacing many things' (5:16).

Thus, Islam is not a new religion with a new Scripture. Instead of being the youngest of the major monotheistic world religions, from a Muslim viewpoint it is the oldest. Islam represents the 'original' as well as the final revelation of the God of Abraham, Moses, Jesus, and Muhammad. The Quran, like the Torah and the Evangel, is based on a preexisting heavenly tablet, the source or mother of Scripture. It is a book written in Arabic that exists in heaven with God; from it, the discourses or teachings of the three Scriptures are revealed at different stages of history: 'Every term has a book ... and with Him is the essence of the Book' (13:38–39).

Since Muslims believe that the Quran's Arabic language and character are revealed (26:195; 41:44), all Muslims, regardless of their national language, memorize and recite the Quran in Arabic whether they fully understand it or not. Arabic is the sacred language of Islam because, in a very real sense, it is the language of God. In contrast to Judaism and Christianity, whose Scriptures were not only translated into Greek and Latin at an early date but also disseminated in vernacular languages, in Islam Arabic has remained the language of the Quran and of religious learning. Until modern times, the Quran was printed only in Arabic; it could not be translated in Muslim countries. Even now, translations are often accompanied by the Arabic text.

Since the Quran is God's book, the text of the Quran, like its author, is regarded as perfect, eternal, and unchangeable. This belief is the basis for the doctrine of the miracle of inimitability of the Quran, which asserts that the ideas, language, and style of the Quran cannot be reproduced. The Quran proclaims that even the combined efforts of human beings and jinns could not produce a comparable text (17:88). The Quran is regarded as the only miracle brought by the Prophet. Muslim tradition is replete with stories of those who converted to Islam on hearing its inimitable message and of those pagan poets who failed the Quranic challenge (10:37–38) to create verses comparable with those contained in the Quran. Indeed, throughout history, many Arab Christians as well have regarded it as the perfection of Arabic language and literature.

In addition to its place as a religious text, the Quran was central to the development of Arabic linguistics and provided the basis for the development of Arabic grammar, vocabulary, and syntax. As Philip K. Hitti observed:

> In length the Koran is no more than four-fifths that of the New Testament, but in use it far exceeds it. Not only is it the basis of the religion, the canon of ethical and moral life, but also the textbook in which the Moslem begins his study of language, science, theology, and jurisprudence. Its literary influence has been incalculable and enduring. The first prose book in Arabic, it set the style for future products. It kept the language uniform. So that whereas today a Moroccan uses a dialect different from that used by an Arabian or an Iraqi, all write in the same style.

Today, crowds fill stadiums and auditoriums throughout the Islamic world for public Quran recitation contests. Chanting of the Quran is an art form. Reciters or chanters are held in an esteem comparable with that of opera stars in the West. Memorization of the entire Quran brings great prestige as well as merit. Recordings of the Quran are enjoyed for their aesthetic as well as their religious value.

Source: John L. Esposito, Islam: The Straight Path *(Oxford: Oxford University Press: 1988), 19–21.*

EXERCISE

1 What extra information do we learn here of the shape and size of the Qur'an?

2 What forms of revelation are recognised in Islam?

3 How does the Qur'an treat previous revelations, such as Jewish and Christian scriptures?

4 How has the Qur'an been important in Arab culture?

DISCUSSION

1 The 114 surahs consist of about 6,000 verses. The earlier surahs, revealed in Mecca (610–622 CE), tend to be shorter than the later surahs, revealed in Medina in the second Meccan period (622–632 CE). Since the surahs are arranged by length, with the longer surahs first, the shorter chapters that were revealed first actually appear later in the text than the longer, later surahs.

2 Three forms of revelation are recognised: nature, history and scripture. Thus the awe and majesty of nature bear witness to the power of God, and the rise and fall of nations according to their obedience to God's messengers.

3 The Torah (Jewish scripture) and Gospel (Christian scripture) are recognised, but the original revelation, which would have been consistent with the Qur'an, is seen as having been corrupted by Jews and Christians. For example, Jesus' original message is seen as having been corrupted by Christians who claim that Jesus is the Son of God (surah 9:30–1). In contrast the Qur'an itself is a final, complete and uncorrupted revelation. The Qur'an thus represents Islam not as a new religion but as the definitive statement of the original revelation that God has made in different ages through different messengers and prophets.

4 The Qur'an has been important in Arabic culture because it defined the written form of the Arabic language, and has remained the

language of scripture across the Muslim world. It has been central to the development of the Arabic language, and its recitation and memorisation are highly esteemed. □

Hearing the Qur'an

EXERCISE

After listening to the 'recitation of the Holy Qur'an' on Audio CD 1, track 24, consider this question:

Why do you think recitation of the Qur'an is so popular in Muslim-majority societies?

DISCUSSION

As Arabic is considered the language of God, Qur'anic recitation enjoys high status as a religious activity as well as having an aesthetic aspect. Furthermore, as Muslims throughout the world hear and recite the Qur'an in Arabic, Qur'anic recitation underlines the universality of Islam and the centrality of the Qur'an. Also, as we discover elsewhere in this module, recitation of sacred texts is common in a variety of religious traditions.

Scholars have described Muslim-majority societies, especially the Arabic speaking world, as 'cultures of secondary orality'. This means that while they do not rely on oral transmission as the sole means of communication, and have written texts (e.g. the Qur'an and *hadith*), oral performance – storytelling, poetry, and the recitation of texts – remains very important. It has been argued that the revival of religious tradition in these cultures has been enabled by the arrival of widely available audio technologies, which provide new channels of sound-based communication. □

READING 5 CONTINUED

Revelation and prophecy

While sharing a belief in revelation and prophecy, Islam's doctrine of prophecy is broader than that of Judaism and Christianity. In addition to prophets, there are messengers from God. Both are divinely inspired, sinless, recipients of God's revelation. However, messengers are given a message for a community in book form and, unlike prophets, are assured success by God. While all messengers are prophets, all prophets are not messengers. The word 'prophet' is applied far more inclusively in Islam than in the Judaeo-Christian traditions. It is applied to Abraham, Noah, Joseph, and John the

Baptist as well as nonbiblical prophets of Arabia like Hud and Salih. 'Messenger' is limited to men like Abraham, Moses, Jesus, and Muhammad who are both prophets and messengers.

The Quran, like the Bible, is a history of prophecy and God's revelation but with fundamental differences. Muslims trace their heritage back to Abraham, or Ibrahim. Thus, Jews, Christians, and Muslims are not only 'People of the Book,' but also Children of Abraham. However, they belong to different branches of the same family. While Jews and Christians are descendants of Abraham and his wife Sarah through their son Isaac, Muslims trace their lineage back to Ismail, Abraham's first-born son by his Egyptian bondswoman, Hagar. Islamic tradition teaches that Abraham, pressured by Sarah who feared that Ismail, as first born, would overshadow Isaac, took Hagar and Ismail to the vicinity of Mecca, where he left them on their own. Ismail became the progenitor of the Arabs in northern Arabia. When Abraham later returned, Ismail helped his father build the Kaba as the first shrine to the one true God. Muslim tradition also holds that it was here at the Kaba that Abraham was to sacrifice his son. In contrast to the biblical tradition (Genesis 22), Islam designates Ismail rather than Isaac as the intended victim, spared by divine intervention.

Islam's doctrine of revelation (*wahy*) also contrasts with that of modern biblical criticism. Both the form and content, as well as the message and actual words of revelation are attributed to an external source, God. Muhammad is merely an instrument or a conduit. He is neither author nor editor of the Quran, but God's intermediary. Traditional teachings, emphasizing that the Prophet was illiterate, that he received the revelation from God through the angel Gabriel, and that even the order of the chapters of the Quran was revealed, may be seen as underscoring the belief that in every sense the Quran is the *literal* word of God with no input from Muhammad.

In Islam, God does not reveal Himself, for God is transcendent, but rather His will or guidance. Revelation occurs through the direct inspiration of prophets or through angelic intercession:

> God speaks to no human except through revelation *wahy* or from behind a veil or He sends a messenger [angel] and reveals whatever he wills ... a straight path, the path of God. (42:51–53)

The Quran was initially preserved in oral and written form during the lifetime of the Prophet. Portions of the revelation were committed to memory by companions of the Prophet as they were received, or were written down by his secretaries. The entire text of the Quran was finally collected in an official, authorized version during the rule of the third caliph, Uthman ibn Affan (reigned 644–56). The Quran was collected, not edited or organized thematically. This format has long proved frustrating to many non-Muslims who find the text disjointed or disorganized from their point of view, since the topic or theme often changes from one paragraph to the next. However, many Muslims believe that the ordering of the chapters and verses was itself divinely inspired. Moreover, this format enables a believer, however brief one's schedule, to simply open the text at random and start reciting at the beginning of any paragraph, since each bears a truth to be learned and remembered.

Source: John L. Esposito, Islam: The Straight Path, *21–3.*

EXERCISE

1 What is the difference between 'messengers' and 'prophets'?

2 How does the Islamic doctrine of revelation (*wahy*) differ from modern biblical criticism?

DISCUSSION

1 Both messengers and prophets are regarded as divinely inspired and sinless, but in addition messengers have received a revealed book, and their success is divinely assured. The latter point has caused particular controversy between Muslims and Christians because Muslims do not accept the crucifixion of Christ, which would be seen as too humiliating an experience for God's messenger. Rather, they claim that a substitute was crucified in Jesus' place, and Jesus was translated directly into heaven.

2 The Islamic doctrine of revelation (*wahy*) differs from modern biblical criticism in that the only role allowed for the recipient of revelation is that of a channel. Muhammad's personality, thoughts and experience, although important for Muslims as an example of human excellence, do not inform the revelation. In contrast, modern biblical scholarship regards the final text of the Bible as the work of editors or 'redactors' (from the German word for editing), whose interests, context and community needs shaped the selection and presentation of the material in the gospels and other biblical texts. □

Major teachings of the Quran

READING 5 CONTINUED

While the Muslim sees but one divine source for the Quran, the non-Muslim will search out human sources and explanations. This is particularly true where parallels exist between Quranic and biblical stories. Christian and Jewish communities did exist in Arabia.

Moreover, Muhammad's travels as a caravan trader brought him into contact with other People of the Book. He would have known and been aware of these forms of monotheism. However, determining the movement from social and mercantile contacts to religious influences and casual connections is difficult. Muslims offer a simple and direct solution. Similarities in revelation and practice are due to their common divine source; differences occur where Judaism and Christianity departed from their original revelation.

If there is a statement of the core doctrines of Islam, it occurs in the fourth chapter of the Quran:

> O believers, believe in God and His Messenger and the Book He has sent down on His Messenger and the Book which He sent down before. Whoever disbelieves in God and His angels and His books, and His messengers, and the Last Day, has surely gone astray into far error. (4:136)

ALLAH

At the center and foundation of Islam is Allah, the God, whose name appears more than 2,500 times in the Quran. In a polytheistic, pagan society Muhammad declared the sole existence of Allah, the transcendent, all-powerful and all-knowing Creator, Sustainer, Ordainer, and Judge of the universe. While God is concerned about mankind, knows people intimately, and can act in history, He is and remains transcendent: 'No vision can grasp Him, but His grasp is over all vision. He is above all comprehension, yet is acquainted with all things' (6:103). Thus; people cannot know God directly. The Quran does not reveal God, but God's will or law for all creation.

The transcendent God is the one God, and He is the only God: 'And your God is one God. There is no god but He' (2:163). God is not a Trinity (5:76); He has no begotten son (2:116) nor daughters nor consorts (6:100–01); and finally, unlike the religion of pre-Islamic Arabia, God has no partners or associate deities (6:22–24).

When Muslims worship five times each day, they declare Islam's absolute or radical monotheism: 'I witness that there is no god but the God (Allah).' Throughout the Quran, God reminds His people that He alone exists and is to be worshipped. This radical monotheism and the consequent iconoclasm of Islam were vividly demonstrated when Muhammad entered the Kaba on his triumphant return to Mecca and destroyed the tribal idols. Its central theological significance is underscored by the Quran's condemnation of associationism or idolatry (associating or allowing anything to usurp God's place) as the great sin (31:13). Indeed it is the one unforgivable sin: 'God forgives not that aught should be associated with Him ... Whoso associates with God anything, has indeed forged a mighty sin' (4:48).

Culturally, this concern not to compromise the unity and transcendence of God led to an absolute ban on any image or representation of God or Muhammad. Many Arab Muslims extended this ban to any representation in art of the human form for fear that such statues and paintings might lead to idol worship. This attitude resulted in the use of calligraphy (Arabic script) and arabesque (geometric and floral design) as dominant forms in Islamic art.

The absolute monotheism of Islam is preserved in the doctrine of the unity and sovereignty of God which dominates Islamic belief and practice. Allah is the one, true God. As God is one, His rule and will or law are comprehensive, extending to all creatures and to all aspects of life. [...] [T]his belief affected early Muslim conceptions and institutions so that religion was viewed as integral to state, law, and society.

The overwhelming sense of God's sovereignty and power is epitomized in the declaration 'God is Most Great' (*Allahu Akbar*), which has served as a preface to the call to prayer and as the traditional battle cry of God's fighters or holy warriors throughout Islamic history, from Muhammad's early battles to contemporary struggles in Iran and Afghanistan.

If God is the Lord, then the Muslim is His servant before whom submission (*islam*) or obedience is the most natural and appropriate response. The term 'Muslim' means 'one who submits' or surrenders to God; it includes everyone who follows His guidance and performs His will. All the great monotheistic prophets are regarded as true Muslims. Thus, Abraham is not a Jew or a Christian but a follower of the true religion, one who submitted (*muslim*) to God (3:67). Is this submission that of a slave before a powerful and fearsome master? Many non-Muslim commentators portray Allah in this way. A careful reading of the Quran and a look at Muslim practice indicate otherwise.

While the Quran, like the Bible, underscores the awesome power and majesty of God and the Day of Judgment, the verses of the Quran reveal a merciful and just judge. Opening the Quran to its initial chapter, one reads, 'In the name of God, the Merciful and Compassionate.' Each of its chapters begins with this appellation, keeping before the believer a reminder of the nature of the God of this revelation. The terms 'merciful' and 'compassionate' are intensive forms of the same root, *rahmat*. This quality or attribute includes the idea not only of forgiveness, but also of a bounteous mercy that sustains, protects, and rewards people. 'Mercy' includes such meanings as the beneficence, compassion, and graciousness of God.

God's mercy permeates the entire life and milieu of the believer. It is reflected in nature, which serves as the theater for the human realization of God's will in history and creation, and reaches its zenith in God's merciful gift to humankind, His revelation.

The Quran declares that everyone experiences the signs of God's mercy in the activities of nature:

> It is He who sends the winds like heralds of glad tidings, going before His Mercy: when they have carried the heavy-laden clouds, We drive them to a land that is dead, make rain to descend thereon, and produce every kind of harvest therewith. (7:57)

The Quran teems with references to the many wonders of nature that God's mercy provides: 'Night and Day that you may rest therein' (28:73); the 'sun and moon follow courses [exactly] computed' (55:5); God provides animals such as cattle and 'from them you derive warmth, and numerous benefits, and of them ye eat ... for your Lord is indeed Most Kind, Most Merciful' (16:5–7); and God created man and made all the earth subject to him (22:65).

While creation and God's dealings with His creatures reflect His Mercy, His beneficence is supremely manifest in His revelation to humankind through the prophets, culminating in the final revelation of the Quran. Its author is the Most Merciful (36:5) in it is mercy (29:51), and its motivation is the mercy of God: 'We sent it down during a blessed night for We (ever) wish to warn (against) evil) ... For we (ever) send (revelation) as a Mercy from your Lord: for He hears and knows (all things)' (44:3–6). Similarly, the sending of Muhammad was a sign of God's mercy: 'We sent you not, but as a Mercy for all creatures' (21:107).

The lesson of God's mercy proclaimed by the Quran has been institutionalized and reinforced by the Muslim practice of beginning important matters such as a letter, public speech, lecture, article, or book with the phrase, 'In the name of God, the Merciful and Compassionate.' No wonder that Muslims take exception to those who describe Muslim faith as primarily based upon fear of a terrible God.

Strong emphasis on God's mercy should not conjure up a permissive deity. God's mercy exists in dialectical tension with His justice. The Quran gives the sobering warning, 'Your Lord is quick in retribution, but He is also oft forgiving, Most Merciful' (7:167). Even here, justice is tempered by mercy toward the repentant sinner. However, sinners, such as those who fall away from the faith, can expect 'the curse of

Allah and the angels and of men combined' (3:86–87). The absolute justice of God and the sinner's inability to escape His retribution (save for repentance) are declared time and again:

> As to those who reject faith, if they had everything on earth, and twice repeated, to give as ransom for the penalty of the Day of Judgment, it would never be accepted of them. Theirs will be to get out therefrom: Their penalty will be one that endures. (5:39–40)

Yet, if the sinner repents of wrongdoing, the Quran assures that 'Allah is Forgiving and Merciful' (5:42).

God's justice is based on the belief that He knows and sees all and that individuals are responsible for each and every action. Reward and punishment follow from individual, ethical responsibility and accountability before an all-knowing and just judge. Thus, Islamic ethics follow from mankind's special status and responsibility on earth.

Source: John L. Esposito, Islam: The Straight Path, *23–6.*

EXERCISE

1 What cultural effects has Islamic monotheism had?

2 How is the relationship between God and the individual believer represented in the Qur'an?

DISCUSSION

1 Monotheism has influenced Muslim material culture because restrictions on visual representations (stricter in some areas than others – especially strict in the Arabian peninsula) resulting from the doctrine of *shirk* have led to greater concentration on calligraphy and abstract forms. It is argued here that the emphasis on the oneness of God and his sovereignty over creation may have militated against dividing up Muslim societies into different spheres of influence, so religion has remained important in law, state and society. However, we should remember from Ruthven, Chapter 1, that the extent to which Islam provides a blueprint for a state, or even for all areas of law, is a hotly contested topic among Muslim believers and scholars.

2 Each individual is accountable before God for his or her own actions. There is a balance between God's role as righteous judge of human wickedness, and his role in providing and caring for humanity, shown in the repeated stress on the virtues of compassion and mercy. □

READING 5 CONTINUED

The Quranic universe

The Quranic universe consists of three realms: heaven, earth, and hell. Governed by its creator-judge, the world is inhabited by human beings and spirits (angels, jinns, and devils) who are called to obedience to the one, true Allah, the Lord of the Universe. Angels serve as the link between God and human beings. Created out of light, immortal and sexless, they function as guardians, recorders, and messengers from God. They are transmitters of God's message, communicating divine revelation to the prophets. Thus, Gabriel (Jibril) brought down the Quran from heaven to Muhammad. Among the more prominent angels are Michael and Israfel. Somewhere between angels and humans are the invisible, intelligent spirits called jinn. In contrast to human beings, the jinn were created from fire instead of earth (7:12, 55:14–15). They have the ability to assume visible form and, like humans, can be good or bad, sin as well as be saved (46:29–31). They will be judged on the Last Day and consigned to paradise or hell. Folk tales such as *The Thousand and One Nights* ascribe magical powers to the jinn, who became known in the West as genies. Finally, at the opposite end of the spectrum from God, the principal of good, is Satan (*shaytan,* adversary), the principal of evil. The origin of Satan goes back to the Garden, where, as will be discussed, one of the angels (Iblis or Satan, the devil) refused to pay homage to Adam. Satan is the leader of other fallen angels and jinn, disobedient servants of God who tempt human beings in their earthly moral struggle on earth. It was Iblis who tempted Adam and Eve (20:116–22). Although permitted by God to engage in their evil ways, Iblis and his followers will be consigned to hell on Judgment Day.

Of all creation, man enjoys a unique relationship with God, for after creating Adam, God breathed into him His spirit (15:29). Moreover, the Quran declares that God created human beings in 'the best of molds or stature' (95:4) to be His representatives on earth. This special selection and status led to Satan's rebellion, a story that strikingly conveys the cosmic significance of humankind.

Informed by God of mankind's special status, the angels initially protested, 'Will You set therein one who will do corruption there, and shed blood, while we proclaim your praise and call You Holy?' (2:30). Adam proved the uniqueness of humankind by demonstrating a God-given knowledge of creation that the angels did not possess. However, when God commanded the angels to prostrate themselves before Adam, Satan or Iblis refused (2:34 and 7:11ff). It was Satan's refusal to accept man's unique status in the hierarchy of the universe that caused his rebellion and expulsion from heaven, and led to the Fall and to the age-long moral struggle of human beings, torn between the forces of good (God) and those of evil (Satan).

> Then the angels bowed all together, except for Iblis who refused to be among those bowing. God said: Iblis, why are you not among those who bow down on their knees? He said: I am not going to kneel before a human being that you have made from clay, from moulded mud. God said: Get out of here; you are an outcast. My curse will be on you until the Day of Judgment! He said: My Lord, let me wait until the Day of Resurrection. God said: You shall be allowed to wait until the appointed time. He said: My Lord, since you have led me astray, I shall make things on the earth attractive to them and lead them astray, except for your sincere servants. God said: This will be a straight path to me. You shall have no authority except over those who are perverse and follow you. Hell shall be their promised place. (15:30–42)

The essence of human uniqueness lies in one's vocation as God's representative on earth. God has given people the earth as a divine trust (33:72); they are thus His viceregents or agents on earth (2:30, 35:39) to whom God has made all creation subservient (16:12–14). It is on the basis of how this viceregency is executed, or how God's will in history is realized or actualized, that a person will be rewarded or punished:

> It is He who has made you (His) agents, inheritors of the earth. He hath raised you in ranks, some above others that He may try you. For thy Lord is quick in punishment, yet He is indeed Oft Forgiving, Most Merciful. (6:165)

It is here that we see the roots of Islamic ethics. God ordains; humankind is to implement His will. Human responsibility and mission are of cosmic proportion, and people will be judged on the cosmic consequences of their acts. As God's representatives, the measure of human actions, and indeed life, is the extent to which the Muslim contributes to the realization of God's will on earth. This responsibility lies squarely on each individual's shoulders, since no one can bear another's responsibility or suffer for another:

> Nor can a bearer of burdens bear another's burden. If one heavily laden should call another to (bear) his load, not the least portion of it can be carried (by the other), even though he be nearly related ... And whosoever purifies himself does so for the benefit of his own soul. (35:18) ... And whatever good you do, you shall not be denied the just reward of it ... As for

> the unbelievers, their riches shall not avail them, neither their children against God; those are the inhabitants of the Fire, dwelling therein forever. (3:115–16)

Although it is not a prominent theme in the Quran, Muslim tradition did come to accept the intercession of Muhammad on behalf of individuals. However, unlike Christianity, there is no vicarious suffering or atonement for humankind. Such actions are unnecessary, since Islam has no doctrine of original sin.

The story of the Fall in the Quran differs from that in the Bible in its teaching regarding personal responsibility. It is Adam, not Eve, who is tempted by the devil. Woman is not portrayed as the cause of the Fall, as in the Judeo-Christian traditions. Moreover, the sin of Adam and Eve is just that – their own personal sin. It is an act of disobedience for which they, and they alone, are responsible. Unlike Christianity, there is no notion of an inherited 'original' sin, committed by the progenitors of the human race, for which all humanity suffers. Sin is not a state of being; it is the result of an act of disobedience, failure to do or not to do what God commands or prohibits. Human beings are not sinful by nature; as they are created or finite creatures, they are naturally limited, weak, and subject to temptation. Similarly, death follows from the human condition and is not due to sin or the Fall. The consequences of sin, like human responsibility, belong solely to those who commit sin.

The biblical and Quranic stories about the consequences of the Fall reveal the basis for the divergent doctrines of Christianity and Islam. The former views the Fall as the cause of man's flawed nature and existence; the latter finds here the story of sin, God's mercy, repentance. In the Bible, the Fall brings a life of shame, disgrace, and hardship:

> To the woman He said, 'I will greatly multiply your pain in childbearing; in pain you shall bring forth children, yet your desire shall be your husband, and he shall rule over you.' And to Adam He said, 'Because you have listened to the voice of your wife, and have eaten of the tree of which I commanded you, you shall not eat of it, cursed is the ground because of you; in toil you shall eat of it all the days of your life; thorns and thistles it shall bring forth to you.' (Genesis 3:16–18)

In sharp contrast, the Quran teaches that after Adam disobeys God but repents, God extends to Adam His mercy and guidance: 'But his Lord chose him. He turned to him and gave him guidance' (20:122). Adam turned away from Satan and sin and turned back to God; Adam repented, and God forgave. This is the paradigm for sin and repentance in Islam. If the Muslim is one who is to submit to God by following His will, sin is disobedience or refusal to submit. It is the arrogance and ingratitude of creatures who forget or turn away from their creator and sustainer. Repentance is simply remembering or returning to God's path, the straight path of Islam. There is little or no emphasis on feelings of shame and disgrace or guilt. What God commands, and what His awesome character engenders, is fear of God (*taqwa*): 'The most honored of you in the sight of God is the most righteous or God fearing of you' (49:13).

Taqwa means self-protection or fear of God. This attitude or disposition follows from belief in an all-powerful, omnipresent God (an ever present God who is as near as one's jugular vein, 50:16), who has commanded submission or obedience to His will and before whom the Muslim is morally responsible and accountable. It is the response of the believer who knows what he or she must do and who lives life ever mindful of the eternal consequences that await on the Last Day. The duties and obligations of Muslim life, as well as its rewards and punishments, fall equally on men and women:

> The believers, men and women, are guardians of one another, they enjoin good and prohibit evil, perform the prayer, give alms, and obey God and His Prophet. (9:71) ... Whoever does a righteous deed, whether man or woman, and has faith, we will give a good life; and we shall reward them according to the best of their actions. (16:97)

Source: John L. Esposito, Islam: The Straight Path, *27–30.*

EXERCISE

1 How is the Qur'anic universe divided up, and what are angels, *jinns* and devils?

2 What is distinctive about humanity?

3 How does the Qur'anic account of the Fall (of humanity) differ from the biblical account?

DISCUSSION

1 There are three realms in the Qur'anic universe: heaven, earth and hell. Angels, *jinns* and devils are spirits who inhabit earth alongside humanity and other physical creatures. Angels mediate between God and humanity – in some traditions, the angel Gabriel (Gibreel or Jibril) is held to have revealed the Qur'an to Muhammad. The *jinns* are invisible spirits who, like humans, are capable of sin and

salvation. Humanity's special status as God's representatives on earth was a cause of jealousy for the angels, resulting in the fall of Satan (*shaytan* or Iblis).

2 Humanity is distinctive in its calling to be God's representatives on earth.

3 The main difference between Qur'anic and biblical accounts seems to be the emphasis on punishment in the latter (which Esposito links to shame and guilt), whereas in the former repentance is followed by forgiveness and guidance. Hence, in Islamic tradition, the episode of the Fall of humanity is not used as the occasion for an explanation of the origins of human hardship and suffering. □

READING 5 CONTINUED

The Muslim community

The Muslim mission to be servants of God and to spread God's rule is both an individual and a community obligation. The Quran emphasizes the social dimension of service to God, for it is on earth and in society that God's will is to govern and prevail. As humankind came from a single pair of parents, so too God 'made you into nations and tribes' (49:13). Similarly, as God had sent His prophets and revelation to the Jews and then to the Christians, He declares in the Quran that the Muslims now constitute the new community of believers who are to be an example to other nations: 'Thus We made you an *umma* justly balanced, that ye might be witness over the nations' (2:143).

Guided by the word of God and the Prophet, the Muslim community has a mission to create a moral social order: 'You are the best community evolved for mankind, enjoying what is right and forbidding what is wrong' (3:110). This command has influenced Muslim practice throughout the centuries, providing a rationale for political and moral activism. Government regulations, Islamic laws, and the activities of religious police who monitor public behaviour have all been justified as expressions of this moral mission to command the good and prohibit evil. Again, Muhammad and the first Muslim community are seen as exemplifying this ideal, implementing the socially just society envisioned by the Quran.

While recognizing differences in status, wealth, and tribal origin, the Quran teaches the ultimate supratribal (transnational) unity and equality of all believers before God. Common faith, not tribal or family ties, binds the community. The Quran envisions a society based on the unity and equality of believers, a society in which moral and social justice will counterbalance oppression of the weak and economic exploitation. Belief and action are to be joined; Muslims are not only to know and believe, but also to act and implement. Worship and devotion to God embrace both private and public life, affecting not only prayer, fasting, and pilgrimage, but social behaviour as well. Like his prophetic predecessors, Muhammad brought a revelation that challenged the established order. The message of the Quran was reformist, if not revolutionary. Quranic prescriptions would provide the basis for the later development of Islamic law to chart this new social order. The scope of Quranic concerns reflects the comprehensiveness of Islam. It includes rules concerning modesty, marriage, divorce, inheritance, feuding, intoxicants, gambling, diet, theft, murder, fornication, and adultery.

The socioeconomic reforms of the Quran are among its most striking features. Exploitation of the poor, weak, widows, women, orphans (4:2; 4:12), and slaves is vividly condemned:

> Those who live off orphans' property without having any right to do so will only suck up fire into their bellies, and they will roast in the fires (of hell). (4:10)

False contracts, bribery, abuse of women, hoarding of wealth to the exclusion of its subordination to higher ends, and usury are denounced. The Quran demands that Muslims pursue a path of social justice, rooted in the recognition that the earth belongs ultimately to God and that human beings are its caretakers. While the wealth is seen as good, a sign of hard work and God's pleasure, its pursuit and accumulation are limited by God's law. Its rewards are subject to social responsibility toward other members of the community, in particular the poor and needy:

> The alms (*zakat*) are for the poor and needy, those who work to collect them, those whose hearts are to be reconciled, the ransoming of slaves and debtors, and for the cause of God, and for travellers. (9:60)

Social justice was institutionalized by Quranic decrees that required the payment of an alms tax (*zakat*) and a voluntary charity for the poor, stipulations of fixed shares of inheritance for women and children, and a host of regulations regarding the just treatment of debtors, widows, the poor, orphans (90:13–16), and slaves (24:33). Those who practice usury are sternly rebuked and warned that they face 'war from God and His prophet' (2:279).

Source: John L. Esposito, Islam: The Straight Path, *30–1.*

EXERCISE

What guidance for the conduct of the Muslim community does the Qur'an provide?

DISCUSSION

There is a strong social dimension to service to God. Much emphasis has been placed on surah 2:143, which calls on the Muslim community to pursue and encourage what is right and forbid what is bad. Specific regulations cover dress, marriage, divorce, inheritance, feuding, alcohol, gambling, diet, theft, murder and sex outside marriage. There are measures to protect vulnerable people such as widows, orphans, women and slaves, and *zakat* (alms for the needy) has become one of the Five Pillars of Islam. ☐

READING 5 CONTINUED

The last day

While Muslims are exhorted to follow God's will out of obedience and gratitude to their creator, the specter of the Last Judgment, with its eternal reward and punishment, remains a constant reminder of the ultimate consequences of each life. It underscores the Quran's strong and repeated emphasis on the ultimate moral responsibility and accountability of each believer. At a moment known only to God, all will be called to judgment in a great cosmic cataclysmic event (81:1–14), also referred to as the Day of Decision or the Day of Reckoning. Each community will be judged by the standards brought by its prophets and Book. Humans and jinn (spirits) alike will stand before the throne of God. All are responsible for their own actions and will be judged according to the record found in the Book of Deeds (45:29–30). As discussed previously, there is no redemption, atonement, or intercession through an intermediary. Allah, who is a merciful but all-powerful judge, consigns all either to heaven or to hell as He wills (5:43). While the Quran teaches that intercession belongs to God alone (39:44; 6:54, 70), belief in Muhammad's role as a divinely designated intercessor did develop and was justified by the text, 'There is no intercessor (with God) unless He gives permission' (10:3).

The Quranic vision of the afterlife is both spiritual and physical. Since the Last Day will be accompanied by bodily resurrection (41:39–40, 49–50), the pleasure of heaven and the pain of hell will be fully experienced. The Garden of Paradise is a heavenly mansion of perpetual peace and bliss with flowing rivers, beautiful gardens, and the enjoyment of one's spouses and beautiful, dark-eyed female companions (*houris*). Descriptions of heavenly bliss follow from the general tenor of the Quran, which is life-affirming, emphasizing the beauty of creation and enjoyment of its pleasures within the limits set by God [...]. The Quran offers vivid descriptions of the delights and pleasures of Paradise, seeing no contradiction between enjoyment of both the beatific vision and the fruits of creation:

> in gardens of bliss ... a multitude will be seated on couches set close together ... Immortal youths will serve them with goblets, pitchers and cups filled with water from a spring which will not upset them or dull their senses; and they may choose fruit of any kind and whatever fowl they desire and chaste companions with eyes of beauty like pearls hidden in shells ... We formed them perfectly and made them spotless virgins, chastely amorous and of the same age. (56:12–37)

In sharp contrast, the damned will be banished to hell, forever separated from God. Anguish and despair will be coupled with physical torment, for they will experience

> a fire whose sheets encompass them. If they should ask for relief, then water like molten copper shall be showered upon them to scald their faces. How awful is such a drink and how evil a resting place. (18:29)

Conclusion

For Muslims throughout the centuries, the message of the Quran and the example of the Prophet Muhammad have constituted the formative and enduring foundation of faith and belief. They have served as the basic sources of Islamic law and the reference points for daily life. Muslims today, as in the past, continue to affirm that the Quran is the literal word of God, the Creator's immutable guidance for an otherwise transient world. This transhistorical significance is rooted in the belief that the Book and the Prophet provide external principles and norms on which Muslim life, both individual and collective, is to be patterned. The challenge for each generation of believers has been the continued formulation, appropriation, and implementation of Islam in history. Islamic history and civilization provide the record of that struggle to interpret and to follow the Straight Path.

Source: John L. Esposito, Islam: The Straight Path, *31–3.*

EXERCISE

What does the Qur'an teach about the 'last day' and the afterlife?

DISCUSSION

Surah 81:1–14 depicts Judgment Day, when the world as we know it will be drawn to an end and all who have ever lived judged according to their deeds, as recorded in the Book of Deeds (45:29–30), and consigned to heaven or hell. Judgment Day entails a physical resurrection of the body as well as the spirit, and both the pleasures of heaven and pains of hell are sensually depicted (56:12–37; 18:29). □

We have now completed a brief tour of some of the main teachings of the Qur'an.

5
Islamic visual and material culture

Calligraphy beyond the page

As the word of God, the words of the Qur'an are held in the highest esteem by Muslims, an esteem that extends to the exquisite handwriting in which they have been recorded. Calligraphy has a special place in Islamic culture: most Muslims believe the Qur'an to be the literal words of God (Allah), and these were written down from a very early stage in Muslim history. The development of beautiful script to convey the words of God was also early, and these scripts were often incorporated into decoration on buildings, especially mosques, where Muslims gather to pray. This section takes the form of a visual essay, referring to the colour plates in this study guide. In it we will look at the creative ways in which calligraphy has been used as decoration in a variety of contexts beyond the page.

Qur'anic verses are often used decoratively in mosques, like the tile in Plate 3 from the Fatih mosque in Istanbul (now in Turkey, but then capital of the Ottoman Empire), which was built between 1463 and 1470 CE. Plate 4 shows both Arabic decorative calligraphy and translations of the 'Bismillah' and other Qur'anic verses written in Arabic, Urdu and Farsi at a shrine in Pakistan. In Plate 5 we see how calligraphic decoration has been extended colourfully over large areas of mosque exteriors, as with this seventeenth-century mosque from Isfahan, in modern-day Iran, then part of the Persian Empire.

Beyond the mosque, calligraphy is used in many decorative items for domestic use and enjoyment, appearing on textiles, brassware and ceramics, and is employed by contemporary Islamic artists such as British-based Ahmed Moustafa, who created the painting 'The ninety-nine names of God' for the St Mungo Museum of Religious Life and Art in Glasgow. From now on, consciously try to notice how calligraphy is used decoratively in a variety of contexts shown on the DVD and in other Islamic material culture you encounter.

Representational art

It has been suggested that the development of calligraphy as an art form depended in part on Islamic restrictions on the pictorial representation of people and animals. In fact, such representation is not banned in the Qur'an, and, in various periods and places, representational art has flourished in Islamic contexts. We have already encountered contemporary examples of the importance of images for some Muslims in connection with the *hajj* paintings in Egypt (Plates 1 and 2).

The problems associated with representational art largely tend to relate to the dangers of *shirk*, sometimes translated as 'idolatry', but literally meaning 'sharing': it is forbidden to associate anything with God, because God is so far above creation. Thus, not only would any attempt to represent God be completely out of the question, but many have felt that to represent God's creatures would also be inappropriate.

The restriction on creating images has been strongest in the Arabian peninsula, and given the contemporary influence of some highly conservative Arab and Islamist groups and teachers, there is a widespread perception that any sort of representational art is forbidden in Islam. Indeed, it was recently reported that one imam has condemned the use of emoticons (symbols such as 'smiley faces' ☺ used in email and telephone text messages) as 'unislamic'.

Nevertheless, as Islamic art expert Eva Baer points out: 'Notwithstanding the predilection of Muslim artists for abstract designs and the tendency to stress the decorative elements of a picture or its illusory character, literary texts and visual sources quite early reveal a concern with figural art' (Baer, 2004, 1).

Human figures are represented in Islamic contexts in Syria, Mesopotamia and Egypt from the later seventh century CE, and much can be learned about religious observance, daily life, material culture and dress from the vivid scenes and portraits produced in periods of great artistic endeavour under the patronage of, for example, the Muslim Mughal dynasty in northern India (particularly between the sixteenth and eighteenth centuries CE), the Ottoman Empire (which from 1453 had its capital in Istanbul) especially from the latter half of the fifteenth until the late nineteenth century CE, and the Qajar dynasty in Persia (present-day Iran) in the nineteenth century. Undoubtedly much of the portraiture produced in Mughal, Ottoman and Qajar contexts – as so frequently in other milieux – served to confirm ancestry and stress rank and possessions. (It could be argued that the Egyptian house paintings such as those shown in Plates 1 and 2 were also concerned with status, but in this respect religious status – namely that of *hajji/hajja*.) Rather than looking at such stylised formal pictures of rulers, we have chosen two examples that give a flavour of the richness and variety of the artistic traditions of a number of Muslim-majority cultures.

EXERCISE

As you look at the next two pictures (Plates 6 and 7) from different eras and places, think about what strikes you as distinctive about them. Think about the use of colour, how realistic or otherwise they appear, whether you have encountered similar pictures before, and what (if anything) surprised you about them.

DISCUSSION

As we see in Plate 6, which depicts the circumcision ceremony of Emperor Akbar's sons, *c.* 1605, Mughal painting is exceptionally detailed, highly decorative and colourful. As well as recording a significant religious and life-cycle event in the life of the imperial family, we are given an insight into palace life, architecture, costume and social relations. Notice how, although the figures are realistically portrayed, the picture's perspective allows us to see inside and outside simultaneously, so that we can see domestic detail and what is going on behind the walls in relation to the outside world. The beautiful Qajar picture 'A Young Woman with a White Veil' (Plate 7) gives us an insight into court life and women's dress in the private sphere in nineteenth-century Persia, with detailed depiction of richly decorated fabric and jewellery. We should remember that although there have been certain standards of female modesty in the public domain in various Islamic contexts (as we will explore later), that has not negated richly decorated and colourful clothing – frequently influenced by Western fashion – in private or all-female settings. ☐

It is interesting to note that even in areas or traditions where representational art is restricted or absent, photographic images have been widely accepted, from photograph portraits of the Saudi royal family to posters and placards bearing pictures of Ayatollah Khomeini (e.g. Ruthven, 2012, 78) or Osama bin Laden. It seems that 'scientific' representation is acceptable in a way that the efforts of a human artist are not. Art recording the human form may be regarded as creation, and therefore arouse concerns about *shirk*, in a way that photography does not.

This brief look at representational art in Islamic contexts has been included to counter the common assertion that there is no such thing, and to bring to attention art that is often unfamiliar in a Western context. Probably the most common response to the magnificent exhibition 'The Turks' at the Royal Academy, London in 2005, was amazement at the quantity and sheer beauty of the representational art displayed.

No matter what some contemporary Muslims feel about it, over the centuries and to the present day there has been a strong and vibrant tradition of figural art in a variety of Muslim-majority societies. In some ways, the different attitudes to representational art – past and present – reflect the tensions already discussed in deciding who or what is, or is not, 'really' Islamic, and who has the authority to judge that.

Not only has art in Islamic contexts been influenced by various traditions (pre-Islamic middle eastern, Buddhist, Christian, Hindu and Indian regional art, and Western portraiture), but it has in turn influenced other traditions. To ignore that artistic heritage is to neglect an important aspect of visual and material culture in various parts of the Islamic world.

Depicting the Prophet

We do not consider all art produced in Christian-majority contexts – past and present – to be 'Christian art': we tend to reserve that label for art with clearly religious content or intent. Similarly, it is clear that art produced in Islamic contexts is not necessarily 'Islamic' or religious in content and intent. Nevertheless, there has also been – and continues to be – art specifically recording Qur'anic events and significant figures in the history of Islam, including the Prophet himself. This can be a difficult topic to address, as there are such sensitivities surrounding it, and it highlights some of the tensions and issues inherent in the difference between studying and practising religion.

Some Muslims might find the idea of art representing the Prophet shocking and inappropriate, because of concerns about *shirk* and representational art in general. Other arguments against depicting Muhammad would be the impossibility of producing an accurate portrait, or of doing justice to one so special. Conversely, though, it could be argued that Islam so clearly and consistently stresses that Muhammad is not God that there is no danger of idolatry, and thus that neither the status of the Prophet, nor of God, could be compromised by depictions of Muhammad.

Certainly Muslim artists and artists in Muslim-majority contexts have produced pictures of Muhammad, and in some ways this is not surprising, given the level of detail there is about the Prophet (and his appearance) in the Qur'an and the *hadith* literature. A mid-sixteenth-century Turkish manuscript illustration from the *Royal Book of the House of Osman* shows 'The Prophet with His Companions in a Mosque' (Plate 8); angels look down upon the scene. There are a number of illustrated manuscript copies of *The Life of the Prophet* (*Siyer el–nebi*) written by Mustafa ibn Yusuf Zarir of Erzurum in 1388 CE. In Plate 9 we may see how an artist has tried to reach a compromise position in an early seventeenth-century Turkish version of the *Life* by depicting Muhammad as a human figure, surrounded by flame (a sign of holiness, similar to the use of the halo in Christian art), but also with a veiled face. Here the prophet is again shown with his companions, bearing standards.

EXERCISE

Look at Plate 10 which appears in an early fourteenth-century manuscript of Rashid al-Din's *Universal History* from Tabriz. This picture appeared in the first edition of *Islam: A Very Short Introduction*. Now read the boxed text on Ruthven, pages 42–3, and then listen to Malise Ruthven's account on Audio CD 1, track 28, of how the picture came to be dropped from the second edition.

1 Why was the picture left out of the second edition?

2 What do you learn about the difficulties of studying religion from this incident?

DISCUSSION

1 The picture was withdrawn from the second edition as a result of protests from some Muslims who regarded the picture as blasphemous.

2 This incident highlights the difference between studying and practising a religion, and the different, possibly competing, perspectives employed. In this case we see that it can be difficult for scholars to present aspects of a religion with which some adherents are uncomfortable or against which some are strongly opposed.

On the one hand, nobody wishes to cause offence. On the other hand, if something has occurred in the past which some say has never happened, if some aspect which was previously acceptable is now unacceptable, or if something is acceptable to some but not others, the scholar's duty is to present the full picture, not least to demonstrate internal diversity, and to show how a tradition changes and adapts over time. □

6
The *Sira* (biography) of Muhammad

Now we return to Ruthven (2012) to find out more about the context in which the Qur'an was revealed in the life and deeds of Muhammad.

Muhammad is only mentioned four times in the Qur'an, and the Qur'an's style and structure make it difficult to interpret without reference to the context to which the revelation refers. This contextual knowledge is supplied by *hadiths* (traditions) which relate the words of the Prophet and his companions. The period between the start of Muhammad receiving revelations and his death (610–632 CE) falls into two distinct phases. The first, 610–622, was spent in Mecca, building up a small community of believers, often in the face of considerable opposition. This opposition sprang up because the uncompromising monotheism of the Qur'an challenged the pagan images worshipped in the city, and its criticisms of the exploitation of the vulnerable challenged the social status quo. Muhammad sent some of his followers to Abyssinia (now Ethiopia) to escape this early persecution, and their protection by Abyssinia's Christian rulers set a positive early precedent for Muslim–Christian relations. By 622 the situation in Mecca had deteriorated so badly that Muhammad decided to leave, attracted to Medina some 275 miles to the north by an offer to mediate in disputes between tribes in the city. This was to prove a decisive turning point in the political fortunes of the community, and the emigration (*hijrah*) from Mecca to Medina has come to mark the beginning of the Islamic calendar – 'year zero' for the new independent Muslim community which, under Muhammad's leadership, soon established itself as the dominant force in Medina, and was eventually to return in triumph to Mecca.

Now turn to the section of Ruthven, Chapter 2, called '*Sira* (biography)'.

EXERCISE

As you study this section, keep a record of key dates in the development of the Muslim community as they crop up.

Read Ruthven, Chapter 2, pages 36 and 37 (to the end of the second paragraph). For what purposes and when were the first biographies of Muhammad compiled?

DISCUSSION

The first biography was composed by Ibn Ishaq, who died in 767 CE, so it was probably written down at least a century after Muhammad's death (632 CE). Other biographies are even later – ninth and tenth centuries CE. So there was a long period of oral transmission, which has led some to question the accuracy and origins of the material. They were compiled from *hadith*, traditions recording the sayings and actions of Muhammad and his followers. They were compiled for 'exegetical' reasons (to do with explaining the meaning of a text; in this case the Qur'an), and for 'apologetic' reasons (to explain, justify and recommend a particular cause; in this case the Islamic faith). ☐

The new revelation and its relation to past tradition

EXERCISE

Please read Ruthven, pages 37 to 42 (to the end of the first paragraph).

1. According to Muslim tradition, what is the origin of the Ka'ba, and how is its significance for Muslim tradition now marked? (Look in particular at Ruthven, page 38 and Figure 1 on page 24.)
2. In what circumstances did Muhammad first begin receiving revelations? How did he initially respond to these experiences? (Ruthven, 2012, 39–40)
3. What happened in the event of the 'Satanic Verses'? (Ruthven, 2012, 41)

DISCUSSION

1. Muslims believe the Ka'ba was built by Ibrahim (Abraham) near the place where he offered to sacrifice Isma'il, his son with Hagar, who became the ancestor of the Arab people. The event is commemorated by Muslims at *'Id al-Adha* (the Feast of the Sacrifice), the climax of the annual pilgrimage or *hajj*, which takes place just outside Mecca. As noted on p. 23, before and after the *hajj* itself (the greater pilgrimage), Muslims walk around the Ka'ba, following a ritual set up by Muhammad during his final year in Mecca (631–2). The Ka'ba is also the location in Mecca towards which Muslims pray. The photograph shown in Ruthven, Figure 1, shows the black silk covering on the Ka'ba, which is replaced annually.
2. Muhammad first began receiving revelations after a period of reflection and meditation in a cave on Mount Hira near Medina.

He restricted knowledge of these experiences to his close family for three years, until God commanded him to preach publicly.

3 This event, the source for which is Tabari (*d.* 923; Ruthven, 2012, 37), refers to a revelation received by Muhammad during the first Meccan period, which seemed to recognise three Meccan goddesses ('high flying cranes', 41) as intercessors (mediators in prayer) to Allah. However, a fresh revelation was received – which now stands in the Qur'an – that no such authority had been given to these goddesses, and the original verse was attributed to Satanic interference in the process of revelation. Hence the term 'Satanic Verses'. ☐

The *hijrah*, and development of relations with Jewish tribes

EXERCISE

Please read Ruthven, pages 42 to 47 (up to 'Hadith "traditions"').

1 Why did Muhammad and his followers emigrate to Yathrib (later Medina)?

2 How did Muhammad's relationship with the Jews change during his time in Medina, and what consequences did this have?

3 After Muhammad's return to Mecca, how did the Muslim community's relations with non-believers change?

DISCUSSION

1 Muhammad's criticisms of idolatry and injustices in Mecca led to attacks on his early followers, and after the death of two of his closest supporters (his first wife Khadija and his uncle Abu Talib), he decided to accept an invitation to meditate in a dispute in Yathrib, and emigrated there (in 622 CE).

2 After an initially positive relationship, which included treaties recognising their right to autonomy, their common descent from Abraham/Ibrahim, and their monotheism and status as 'people of a book', relations deteriorated. The Jewish rejection of Muhammad as Prophet was crucial, but Muhammad's victory over the ruling Meccan tribe, the Quraish, at the battle of Badr (624 CE) was an important turning point, because this greatly increased his capacity to quell dissent. During the following few years, disputes with the Jewish tribes in the inter-tribal alliance that Muhammad was developing, led

to their expulsion or massacre. Increased distinction also developed at a religious level – for example, the direction of prayer changed from Jerusalem (sacred to Jews) to Mecca, and the Qur'an came to be viewed as a book to rival (and supersede) the Jewish Torah and Christian *Injil* (Gospel).

3 Muhammad's triumph in Mecca removed the compromise element in his relationships with resisting Arab tribes. Where previously he had been prepared to enter truces with them, they were now faced with the choice of submission to Islam or risk of death. Symbolically, the link to the pagan cycle of annual festivals was broken by removing the extra month that had previously been inserted into the calendar to keep it in phase with the seasons. ☐

EXERCISE

Read Ruthven, pages 47 to 51 ('Hadith "traditions"').

How was the *hadith* material been transmitted, and what criteria have been used to assess its reliability?

DISCUSSION

The *hadiths* were passed down orally, and brought together in written form in collections in the ninth century CE. Six such collections became recognised, of which those of al-Bukhari and al-Hajjaj are considered most authoritative. Those collecting the sayings were aware of their varying reliability, and graded their reliability from 'sound' through to 'weak'. To arrive at these judgements they made an investigation into information available about the character of those in the chain of transmission (*isnad*). However, critical scholarship has raised doubts about the reliability of some of these chains – for example, cases where *hadith* were not quoted in early legal discussions where they would have been relevant. The story on pages 50 and 51 indicates that the issue of the authenticity of the *hadiths* was of great importance in early Muslim history, because so much of the *shari'a* is derived from this source. ☐

At the start of this section you were asked to note the dates of some of the key events in Islamic history. Here is my list, to compare with yours:

c. 570 CE	birth of Muhammad
595	Muhammad marries Khadija
610	Muhammad receives first revelation
613	first public preaching
622	Hijra – emigration to Yathrib (Medina)
624	Battle of Badr
630	Muhammad returns triumphant to Mecca
632	death of Muhammad, cessation of revelations

The Prophet in tradition and modernity

EXERCISE

Although its commemoration is not a religious requirement, the Prophet's birthday is widely celebrated through much of the Muslim world. The film of 'Muhammad's Birthday' on the DVD shows these celebrations in Egypt, and features children's views of the importance of Muhammad's example for their lives today. Watch the film now and consider the following question:

What does celebrating Muhammad's birthday mean for these children?

DISCUSSION

The children's statements stress that Muhammad is an example to follow. The boy speaks of Muhammad's bravery and strength, the girl of his qualities and good manners. □

EXERCISE

Read Ruthven, pages 51 to 56 ('The elaboration of Muhammad's image').

How has the image and role of Muhammad been developed in Muslim tradition?

DISCUSSION

In spite of some of the restrictions on visual representation, a very detailed picture of Muhammad is presented in the *hadith* literature, and each detail of his life – down to his clothes, hair style and diet – is held to be an example for the believer to imitate, as the text from al-Ghazali (in Ruthven, the box on page 54) illustrates. He is believed to be sinless, and many miraculous events are associated with him in the *sira*, including splitting the moon, breathing life into a clay bird, and miraculously feeding crowds.

Having examined the role of Muhammad in Muslim tradition as explained by Ruthven, we now consider what Muhammad means for Muslims today, using three short readings. The first of these, Reading 6, comes from Shabbir Akhtar, a British Muslim of South Asian background who was living in Bradford at the time of the controversy over the novel *The Satanic Verses* (1988) by Salman Rushdie (another British South Asian from a Muslim background). The novel used the episode of the 'Satanic Verses' in the *hadith* literature (as discussed above) to explore issues of prophetic inspiration, traditions about Muhammad, and contemporary politics, all from a satirical point of view. The portrayal of Muhammad was regarded by many Muslims as offensive. Passages were circulated in mosques, and there were calls for the book to be reissued with an explanation that it was not intended as an accurate portrayal of the Prophet, which later escalated into calls for it to be banned. In Bradford in January 1989 the book was publicly burned, and in February of that year Ayatollah Khomeini of Iran issued a *fatwa* (legal opinion) declaring Rushdie an apostate (someone who has abandoned and then turned against Islam), who hence ought to be put to death; subsequently a reward was offered for his killing. Rushdie went into hiding and remained in this condition until the late 1990s when, several years after the death of Khomeini, a reforming Iranian government distanced itself from the *fatwa*.

In understanding these events it is important to distinguish between British Muslim indignation at the portrayal of Muhammad and the actions of Khomeini. As a Shi'ite Iranian leader, Khomeini did not represent the views of British Muslims, most of whom are Sunnis and have South Asian (Indian, Pakistani, Bangladeshi) backgrounds. Interviewed in 1989, a Muslim woman in Bradford explained:

> I do not want to see Salman die, that is immoral and wrong, and anyway not what the majority Muslim population here [in Bradford] want. I don't even think the book should be banned. But right from the beginning, I have felt that everyone was treating the Muslim protest as if it was completely crazy. This freedom of expression – why do we have pornography and

> libel laws, and a law of blasphemy which applies only to Christianity? How can that be fair?
>
> (quoted in Alibhai, 1989, 12)

Shabbir Akhtar's book, *Be Careful with Muhammad*, published in 1989, seeks to explain British Muslim indignation and anger, first at the novel, but then more importantly at being viewed as 'completely crazy' in the British press and by much of the British public. He does so by first explaining why respect for Muhammad is so important to Muslims.

In contrast to the traditional Muslim opinions that Akhtar seeks to represent, the other two extracts (Readings 7 and 8) are critiques introducing the work of individual Muslim writers who have sought to champion Islam, but at the same time integrate Islamic thought with various currents in modern thought and aspects of contemporary life. The first writer, 'Abd al-Rahman 'Azzam (henceforward 'Azzam), was an Egyptian diplomat and politician in the mid-twentieth century. He portrays Muhammad as an exemplar for modern international relations. The second, Fatima Mernissi, is a Moroccan sociologist and feminist activist, whose interpretations of the role of women in the life of Muhammad challenge some contemporary attitudes.

READING 6

Be careful with Muhammad

Preface

An illiterate woman in Bradford went to see her teenage daughter's schoolteacher, who said to her: '*The Satanic Verses* is brilliant! In Britain we like to read great literature.' She remained silent and returned home. This book is an attempt to explain that inarticulate believer's anguish. If it achieves anything more, it will be a bonus.

[...]

Shabbir Akhtar, Bradford, August 1989

Epigraph

> 'Believers! Be resolute in the doing of justice, as witnesses to God, even though it be against your own souls, your parents or your relatives, and whether it concerns the rich or the poor. For in the eyes of God neither wealth nor poverty carry any weight. Do not follow your own desires and thereby pervert the truth. Yet if you decide to act in bias and prejudice, God is well aware of the things you do.'
>
> Koran, *The Women*, v. 135

NOTE It is customary for Muslim writers to place the pious expression 'Peace be upon him' after every mention of the name Muhammad, especially in devotional contexts. The author hopes that it does not seem unduly irreverent to omit this expression in a primarily argumentative work.

1 Be careful with Muhammad!

'Say what you like about God – but be careful with Muhammad!' is an old slogan of Western caution about Islam, but one which we might well take seriously in the wake of the controversy surrounding the publication of Salman Rushdie's *The Satanic Verses*. The missionaries and other Christians who preached the Gospel in Islamic lands often found Muslims to be obstinate in their religious convictions and protective about their Prophet. While Muslims tended to accept some forms of satire or parody of the divine ways, they rarely tolerated insults to Muhammad and his family. Belief in God was common to Jews, Christians and Muslims. But endorsement of Muhammad's prophethood was the distinguishing feature of the Muslim outlook. It was the responsibility of Muslims, therefore, to guard the honour of *their* Prophet, the Arabian messenger who had brought them guidance from God.

Salman Rushdie's *The Satanic Verses* is seen by Muslims as a calculated attempt to vilify and slander the Prophet of Islam. Not only has Rushdie said what he pleased about God, he has also taken liberties with Muhammad. The reaction of the Muslim communities world-wide has been loud and clear. The only recent event to have triggered off Muslim emotion on a scale even remotely comparable to the Rushdie affair was the attempt to destroy the al-Aqsa mosque in Jerusalem two decades ago. It will not be our task here to recall all the many dimensions of the Rushdie saga that have crowded the world's headlines for many months. But it will be our task to see why so many Muslims have been willing to spill much more than merely ink over *The Satanic Verses*.

Muhammad ibn Abdullah is, on every score of influence and achievement, a decisive figure in the history of theistic religion. His contribution to the human quest for the holy cannot be reasonably denied. Even so, someone might wonder, why the caution? Why should one be careful with Muhammad? Is he any different from any other historical figure? After all, Moses and Jesus also have vast ideological legacies but the same demand for caution, especially these days, seems unnecessary.

Moses, Jesus and Muhammad are all seminal figures in the history of Western theism. But Muslims jealously guard the reputation of their Prophet in a manner that looks odd even to Jews and Christians, let alone to secularists and rejectors. In the Jewish case, disrespect towards Moses and other Hebrew prophets is tolerated. In fact, blasphemy is restricted to cursing the Lord; insulting Moses is, strictly speaking, not blasphemous: 'Say what you like about Moses – but be careful with God.' As for Jesus, wanton attacks on his personality and the associated Christian convictions have been commonplace in recent decades in secular Western societies. In general, Christians have tolerated these affronts; the character assassination of Jesus has been carried out with impunity.

Muhammad is unique in the respect and honour afforded him by his followers. Though not regarded as divine, Muhammad is held in the highest possible esteem. No pictorial representations are allowed; mention of his name warrants, among the pious, the invocation of divine blessing on him, his family and companions. His wives are seen as the mothers of the faithful. Every detail of his biography has been preserved and countless millions seek to imitate him daily in every aspect of their lives.

The reason for the caution, then, is what may be called 'the posthumous authority of Muhammad'. The influence of the Arabian Prophet on the lives of millions, through the patterns of his biography daily imitated, is without parallel in the whole of history, religious or secular. The imitation of Muhammad is unlike the imitation of Christ, an accepted obligation, a routine occurrence. It is the ideal not only for the saints – but for all Muslims, from the beggars in the slums of India to the spectacularly wealthy sheikhs of Saudi Arabia, from the illiterate peasants of Pakistan to the erudite scholars of al-Azhar, from the village women of the Third World to the sophisticates of Western female society.

Muhammad is dead. But he is dead only in the least significant sense. For he is ideologically alive – and well. The Rushdie affair has demonstrated the extent of Muslim enthusiasm about their messenger and, in doing so, the quality of their allegiance to the ideals he preached. The fact is that the Prophet of Islam is resurrected daily in what must be the greatest triumph over the limitations of physical extinction. It is therefore unsurprising that any attempt to prostitute his reputation should have met with such resolute and uncompromising opposition.

Source: Shabbir Akhtar, Be Careful with Muhammad *(London: Bellew, 1989), vii, 1–3.*

READING 7

'Abd Al-Rahman 'Azzam

'Azzam (1893–1976) was an Egyptian diplomat and served as Secretary-General of the Arab League from 1945 to 1952. In 1938 he wrote an Arabic work entitled *The Hero of Heroes or the most Prominent Attribute of the Prophet Muhammad.* A revised English version was published in 1965 as *The Eternal Message of Muhammad.* The format of the book is worthy of attention. The life of Muhammad itself is briefly sketched in a short twenty pages. Following that are sections dealing with the basic message of Islam, social reform, the state, international relations, dissemination of the message, the causes of world disturbances, and the search for 'a spiritual bulwark for civilization'. The point is clear: Muhammad, through his person and his action, has something to say about each of these aspects of modern (political) existence. Bravery, love, the ability to forgive, and eloquence are all attributes of Muhammad that are emphasized, leading to the conclusion that the diplomatic nature of Muhammad's life is one that provides an example for today in the resolution of conflicts.

> The Message of Muhammad recognizes neither nationalism nor racism in their modern contexts; the fatherland of the Muslim admits of no geographic delimitations – it coexists with the faith ... Racism, or a fanatic attachment to tribe, nation, color, language, or culture, is rejected by the Message as a product of pre-Islamic idolatry.[1]

Political manoeuvres and military insights are also claimed:

> Recognizing the inherent and manifest evils of war, the Message of Muhammad circumscribed warfare with common rules of right conduct (*adab*), defining its aims and limiting it to the repulsion of aggression, the protection of the freedom of belief, and the termination of battle with just and durable agreements ... Certain states nowadays prefer surprise attacks on their enemies without any previous warning. Preliminary precautions prior to attack are such that the aggression-bent state can surprise its enemies completely by pretending all along to favor peace; often the true motives and pretenses for waging war may not be revealed prior to combat ... There is nothing more distasteful to Islam than this, and the tenets of Muslim law reject it in spirit and in practice.[2]

Source: Andrew Rippin (1993) Muslims: Their Religious Beliefs and Practices *(London and New York: Routledge), 56–7.*

[1] Azzam, A. (1965) *The Eternal Message of Muhammad*, New York, Mentor Books, 204–5.

[2] *Ibid.*

READING 8

Fatima Mernissi

A sociologist and university teacher in Morocco, Fatima Mernissi (b. 1940) recently published *Women and Islam: An Historical and Theological Enquiry*, which is as close as one might conceive to being a feminist biography of Muhammad. The root problem of Muslim society today, according to Mernissi, one which the intrusion of the West has forced Muslims to confront, is that women have not been treated as full members of the community.

> Mernissi does not see Islamic gender segregation as an isolated social phenomenon of a religious nature, but as a political expression of a specific distribution of power and authority and an economic reflection of a specific division of labor, both forming a total and coherent social order. When this Islamic segregation is shaken, the coherence of the traditional social order as a whole is put into question, especially if social reform is not able to set up an acceptable new system of values governing male–female relations.[3]

Women may have gained the right to vote in a country such as Morocco, from where Mernissi writes, but they have not gained the right to be elected, she says.[4] Men continue to consider power the privilege of the male and cannot conceive of the need to have women participating in decisions regarding the future. Furthermore, in order to support their position, they appeal to the foundations of the faith of Islam. This accounts for the current surge in Radical Islamist membership, where men find comfort against the inroads of female demands.

To counter these sorts of appeal to religion, Mernissi goes back to the sources to extract a picture of Muhammad as the supporter of women's rights. Mernissi's picture is a mixed one, though. On one level, she seems to say that Islam is inherently male oriented and there is a need to move 'beyond': 'One wonders if a desegregated society, where formerly secluded women have equal rights not only economically but sexually, would be an authentic Muslim society.'[5] But, at the same time, she looks back to Muhammad for inspiration

[3] Boulatta, I. (1990) *Trends and Issues in Contemporary Arab Thought*, Albany, NY, State University Press of New York, 132.

[4] Women can now stand for parliament in Morocco.

[5] Mernissi, F. (1987) *Beyond the Veil: Male–Female Dynamics in Modern Muslim Society*, revised edition, Bloomington, IN, Indiana University Press, 9.

and legitimization. Perhaps this is an attempt to battle Fundamentalist elements (glossed consistently as anti-women) on their own grounds – inter-Muslim apologetics. Muhammad is the champion of women; his opinion is even over-ruled on occasion by God [...] who seems to have been more influenced by the pragmatics of male-oriented power structures than his prophet. The tendency towards reinforcing male power has been further aggravated by male interpreters of the sacred texts, who saw only their own prerogatives at stake and who thought nothing of ignoring Muhammad's intentions of improving the lot of women.

For Mernissi, Muhammad's character reflects precisely what is lacking in contemporary male–female relations:

> Muhammad was a chief of state who publicly acknowledged the importance of affection and sex in life. And, during expeditions, his wives were not just background figures, but shared with him his strategic concerns. He listened to their advice, which was sometimes the deciding factor in thorny negotiations.[6]

The institution of the *hijab*, 'veiling' – here to be taken to mean the entire social system which separates men and women in Muslim countries – became a part of Islam only because of male concerns for their own privileges, and was put in place against the general principles which Muhammad had initiated. Attacks were made on Muhammad because of his private life in which his wives enjoyed a great deal of freedom and authority, contrary to the established practices of society at the time: 'Hurt and weakened, [Muhammad] lost his ability to stand up to 'Umar [pictured here as the spokesman for the male prerogative], and he agreed to the confinement of women. He gave his consent to the *hijab*. He gave his consent to the reestablishment of male supremacy.'[7] Muhammad, for Mernissi, aspired to the ideal society, but the pressures of the situation – a situation into which he had introduced radical change – would not allow his platforms to be maintained. But the equality of men and women and the freedom of women to control their own lives and to be a valuable part of society is what Muhammad stood for, and it is the true core of Islam. The pragmatic value of providing safety for his wives had overcome his principles. Those principles are reflected in the very basis of the religion of Islam, except, it would seem, when it

[6] Mernissi, F. (1991) *Women and Islam: An Historical and Theological Enquiry*, Oxford, Basil Blackwell, 104.

[7] *Ibid.*, 163–4.

comes to dealing with women. Islam, for Mernissi, stands for the use of the intellect as the means by which good is to be separated from evil. The veiling of women imposed the language of violence and power, whereas individual responsibility was the essence of the society which God wished to be instituted. But the ignorant forces of male power could not accept that responsibility.

> Muhammad put great emphasis on politeness. He himself was very shy. Several verses [of the Qur'an] attest to this aspect of his character, which ... in the absence of tactfulness on the part of some men of his entourage forced him to adopt the *hijab*. He did not consider that having a house open to the world had to mean that people would invade his privacy. The *hijab* represented the exact opposite of what he had wanted to bring about. It was the incarnation of the absence of internal control; it was the veiling of the sovereign will, which is the source of good judgment and order in a society.[8]

Source: Andrew Rippin (1993) Muslims: Their Religious Beliefs and Practices *(London and New York: Routledge), 59–61.*

Mernissi's biography is not a traditional one, then. While it covers a great deal of the life of Muhammad, its focus is on the women around him and his attitude towards them. The point of the biography is made explicit to the reader. Indeed, it could well be that, as a result of the rise in general literacy levels, works like that of Mernissi have become more appropriate and more convincing. No longer is it necessary to embed one's idea so deeply in stories.

EXERCISE

For each of these extracts, consider the contemporary significance of the life of the Prophet to the author, or to the community for whom the author claims to write.

DISCUSSION

Akhtar argues that the extent of Muslim reverence for Muhammad is due to the unique extent to which details of his actions are recorded in Muslim tradition and held to be precedents for subsequent Muslim behaviour. There is perhaps a provocation to Christian sensibilities in the sentence: 'The fact is that the Prophet of Islam is resurrected daily in

[8] *Ibid.*, 185.

what must be the greatest triumph over the limitations of physical extinction.'

'Azzam puts a kind of modernist twist on the idea of detailed imitation by presenting Muhammad's rejection of 'tribalism' as a model for the rejection of modern racism and nationalism. Similarly, Muhammad's restraints on the conduct of warfare are made the basis for condemning modern ideas of total war.

Mernissi also sees the example of Muhammad as authoritative, and uses evidence in the *sira* literature of his support for women's autonomy and freedom of action to advocate such practices today – much as 'Azzam does in the field of international politics. In particular, Mernissi argues that 'radical Islamists' are gaining political support because men want to stop women gaining autonomy – a view we shall see partly contested when discussing Ruthven, Chapter 5. But Mernissi's reading is more complex and ambivalent than that of 'Azzam, because through her close readings of the traditions she discerns tensions in the early *ummah*, and even argues that Muhammad was forced against his best intentions to concede to the demands of some male followers and impose the *hijab* on his wives. This portrayal of Muhammad's authority as compromised, and of the earliest Muslim community as the product of political concessions, conflicts with traditional images of the Medinan community as an ideal golden age. □

Mernissi's work arguably illustrates one of the consequences of mass literacy, the spread of communications technologies and erosion of the monopoly of interpretation of Islam previously enjoyed by the '*ulama*: many diverse interpretations of Islam are emerging. Yet diversity is not new to Islam: alongside its emphasis on unity, great diversity has long been part of the tradition. This longstanding tension between unity and diversity, and its many historical manifestations, are the subjects of Ruthven, Chapter 3.

7
Divine unicity

Ruthven, Chapter 3, explores the concept of *tawhid* – 'making one' – a central idea in Muslim thinking, but one that has been developed through much historical diversity. The chapter discusses the division of the *ummah* into Sunni and Shi'a, further sub-divisions of the Shi'a, and disputes and developments (especially Sufism) within Sunni Islam. It examines the particular case of modern Iran, a Shi'a society that underwent an 'Islamic Revolution' under Ayatollah Khomeini in 1979. The unity and diversity of Muslim tradition is further reflected in the historical and regional variety of the mosque, the place of communal prayer for Muslims, which we shall also examine.

Later we shall work through Chapter 4, which looks at the importance of *shari'a* for Muslims. We will consider the historical conditions influencing the formation of this tradition, the sources used to derive it, the challenges and problems of new interpretation, and the ways in which *shari'a* has shaped and now shapes Muslim-majority societies. This will lead us into consideration of two particularly disputed areas of *shari'a* – those relating to women and the family, and to *jihad*.

Now read Ruthven, Chapter 3, '*Tawhid*: introduction', pages 57 to 59, and '*Tawhid* in early Islamic thought', pages 65 to 67.

EXERCISE

1 What was the significance of *tawhid* for the earliest Muslim communities, and how does the Dome on the Rock demonstrate this?

2 What were early theological controversies about, and how were they resolved?

DISCUSSION

1 Ruthven argues that the impulse to 'make one' is central to Islam in all areas of life: in theology, politics and society. The word is not found in the Qur'an but is implicit in the basic statement of Islamic faith, the *shahada*: 'there is no God but God'. For the early Muslim communities it was an emphasis that placed them in continuity with ancient Jewish monotheism, and marked them out from other religions: Zoroastrianism (Persian – a 'dualistic' tradition, accepting two eternal principles of existence: for example, good and evil, light and dark), Christianity (with its 'Trinity' of Father, Son and Holy

Spirit, within the one God), and Arab Paganism (polytheistic, with many gods). The Dome of the Rock in Jerusalem, the earliest surviving substantial man-made Islamic structure, demonstrates this continuity and conflict in its location, architecture and inscriptions. Built on the site of the Jewish temple (destroyed by the Romans in 70 CE) it represents continuity with Judaism. Its domed structure draws on the style of Byzantine Christian churches, but it is larger and situated higher than them, and its inscriptions specifically refute Christian belief in the Trinity.

2 As we saw in Ruthven, Chapter 1, theological controversies have not played a major role in Muslim history, and the *'ulama* tended to discourage theological speculation. Nonetheless, several important debates did take place. One concerned the qualifications for continuing to be called a Muslim. The Khawarij (Kharijites) or Seceders ('those who broke away') argued that a true Muslim must follow the *shari'a*, and anyone who did not should be considered an unbeliever. In contrast, the Murji'a argued that anyone who declares the *shahada* remains a Muslim unless he or she explicitly renounces this commitment – it is up to God, not people, to judge their sins. The Murji'a position has become essentially the mainstream Sunni stance, with the *'ulama* developing ways of distinguishing different degrees of faith, which in turn will be reflected in one's standing in the community.

Another early theological debate concerned free will and predestination. One Qur'anic text that led to argument was surah 111, in which God curses Abu Lahab, the Quraishi leader who opposed Muhammad, condemning him to Hell. As we have seen, traditionalists held that the Qur'an was uncreated – that is eternal with God. Yet if Abu Lahab's condemnation was eternal with God, what free will did Abu Lahab have? Hence some rationalist theologians, the Mu'tazilites, argued that the Qur'an must be created in response to changing situations, rather than eternal with God. However, the Mu'tazilite position became unpopular when the caliph, al-Mamun (reigned 813–33 CE), tried to impose this position forcibly, using an institution called the *mihna*. This was something like the later Christian 'Inquisition', a body backed by the state authorities with the power to try to enforce doctrinal conformity. Later, a former Mu'tazilite called al-Ash'ari worked out a compromise whereby the Qur'an was believed to be uncreated so God does know what everyone is going to do in advance, yet creates the power for people to choose at the moment of decision. This power is acquired from God and in performing the action the individual 'acquires' the moral responsibility for it – hence the doctrine is referred to as the doctrine of 'acquisition'.□

The legacy of the Kharijites: Wahhabism, Saudi Arabia and Islamist extremism

It is important to note that in modern times the Kharijite position has been adopted by some Islamists to justify rebellion against Muslim leaders whom they regard as corrupt. This condemnation of Muslims who reject the Islamist position as unbelievers then legitimises *jihad* (struggle, including violent struggle) against them. In modern times, this doctrine was first revived by the eighteenth-century movement the Wahhabis, in what (since 1932) has been the Kingdom of Saudi Arabia, where Wahhabism is the state religion. It is from this source – especially as a result of Saudi oil wealth from the 1970s enabling the propagation of Wahhabism overseas – that the Kharijite position has spread to Islamist groups.

Shi‘ism: origins and development

Now read Ruthven, ‘The first sectarian divisions’ and ‘Other branches of Shi‘ism’, including the boxed texts, on pages 59 to 65.

EXERCISE

1 What are the origins of Shi‘ism, and how have Hasan and Hussein become models for different kinds of response to the Sunni majority?

2 What minority groups of Shi‘a have developed?

3 What ritual and theology have come to be associated with the death of Hussein?

DISCUSSION

1 The Shi‘a – from *shi‘at Ali*, ‘the party of ‘Ali’ – are those who believe that after Muhammad’s death his role as the spiritual and political leader of the Muslim community should have been taken by ‘Ali, his cousin, son-in-law, and closest male blood relative. Instead, the Muslim elders elected Abu Bakr, the father of Muhammad’s favourite wife ‘Aisha. ‘Ali did eventually become caliph, but only after two other elected leaders, ‘Umar and ‘Uthman. But by this stage rival claims had had time to become established, so that Mu‘awiya, of the Umayyad clan and only distantly related to Muhammad (see the chart of Muhammad’s family in Ruthven, page 59), opposed ‘Ali. ‘Ali offered a compromise, but this was rejected by radicals within his own party, one of whom assassinated him. The Shi‘ite succession then passed to ‘Ali’s oldest son, Hasan, who reached a compromise with Mu‘awiya. But on the latter’s death ‘Ali’s younger son, Hussein,

challenged Mu'awiya's son Yazid, only to be killed in battle by his troops at Karbala, in present-day Iraq. This was to become a defining moment in Shi'ite history and theology. The two sons of 'Ali set two precedents for the Shi'ite relationship with the Sunni majority – one of compromise and coexistence (Hasan), and one of resistance and martyrdom (Hussein).

The direct descendants of 'Ali became known as the Imams, seen by Shi'ites as preserving the dual spiritual and political leadership of Muhammad, but never able to press their claims to successful political resolution. In 750, a Shi'ite-inspired movement succeeded in toppling the Umayyads, leading to the founding of the 'Abbasid dynasty. But these rulers were descended from Muhammad's uncle al-Abbas, not from Muhammad. Meanwhile a number of Imams descended from 'Ali were murdered, until the twelfth one, Muhammad al-Muntazar, it is believed, mysteriously disappeared in 874; he is alive but 'hidden' (in occultation). This disappearance has led to much speculation about when the 'Hidden Imam' – a kind of messiah figure – will return to become the rightful leader of the whole Muslim community. Shi'ites who hold this belief about the twelfth Imam are called Twelver or Imami Shi'ites, and are the largest Shi'ite group, forming the majority population in Iran, Iraq and Bahrain, and with significant minorities elsewhere, including Afghanistan, Pakistan, Syria, Lebanon and India.

2 The Ismail'is and Twelvers split when the Ismai'lis gave their allegiance to Isma'il, the elder son of the sixth Imam, Ja'far al-Sadiq. However, because Isma'il died before his father, Twelvers followed Ja'far's second son, Musa al-Kazim. After Isma'il, the Ismai'li line stems from Isma'il's eldest son, instead of from Ja'far's second son, whom Twelvers believe Ja'far designated as his heir. Between the tenth and twelfth centuries through the Fatimid dynasty, the Ismai'lis ruled an empire in North Africa, centred on Egypt. Contemporary offshoots of the Ismai'lis include the Nizaris, whose leader, the Aga Khan, is the only living imam to be claimed by any Shi'ite group. Other Shi'ite groups include the Druzes of Israel/Palestine, the Alawis of Syria and the Babis of Iran, from whom the Baha'i faith sprang.

3 Both in Karbala, where Hussein was killed (although the practice was restricted under Saddam Hussein), and in many Shi'ite villages, Hussein's 'martyrdom' is re-enacted every year with many participants physically participating in Hussein's suffering by beating themselves in scenes reminiscent of processions of medieval Christian

flagellants. Twelvers also take part in the passion plays described on page 63 of Ruthven.[9] Hussein's death has come to symbolise, and in a mystical sense to embody, the suffering and future redemption of the Shi'a people, rather like the passion of Christ for Christians.

Special authority and knowledge are also ascribed to the Imams, who are believed to hold the key to hidden meanings of scripture. In place of the Hidden Imam, clerics assume his authority, a role that reached its most developed form in Ayatollah Khomeini's doctrine of the 'rule of the *faqih*' (expert in Islamic law). □

Further theological developments in the Sunni and Shi'ite traditions, and Sufism

We have now considered the development of belief in early Islam, Sunni, and Shi'ite, in its historical context. The next passages examine some further theological developments in both traditions. We shall then look at the film on the DVD which shows some of the rituals performed on Ashura, the tenth day of the lunar month of Muharram, when Shi'ites commemorate Hussein's martyrdom at Karbala in Iraq. The footage, shot in 2004, shows Shi'ite Muslims from across the world able to visit Iraq and perform the rituals without restriction for the first time for many years.

We then turn our attention to Sufism, an important devotional and mystical development within Islam, to continue our exploration of Muslim diversity.

Read Ruthven, 'The Sunni consensus' and 'Theosophical speculations', on pages 67 to 70.

EXERCISE

1 What kind of religious authority was exercised by the Sunni *'ulama*?

2 How did Neoplatonism influence Islamic thought, and what kind of Qur'anic interpretation developed under the Ismai'lis?

DISCUSSION

1 After the 'Abbasid caliph Al-Mamun's unpopular attempt to impose Mu'tazilite rationalism, in Sunni Islam religious leadership was largely left to the *'ulama*. Their expertise was text-based rather than

[9] References to Shi'ites and Shi'ism from now on are specifically to Imamis/Twelvers, not the Shi'ite traditions as a whole.

Plate 1 *Hajj* mural painting, El Kurna. From Ann Parker and Avon Neal, *Hajj Paintings: Folk Art of the Great Pilgrimage*, Smithsonian Institution Press, 1995. © Ann Parker.

Plate 2 *Hajja* pictured in front of a mural painting. From Ann Parker and Avon Neal, *Hajj Paintings: Folk Art of the Great Pilgrimage*, Smithsonian Institution Press, 1995. © Ann Parker.

Plate 3 Tile panel above a window in the portico of the Fatih Mosque, Istanbul, 1463–70. The Kufic inscription includes part of the 'Throne Verse'. Photo: © Bernard O'Kane.

Plate 4 The 'Bismillah' and other Qur'anic verses written in Arabic, Urdu and Farsi at a shrine in Pakistan. Photo: World Religions Photo Library.

Plate 5 The Masjid-i Shah, Isfahan built by Shah Abbas, 1612–37. © Josephine Powell, courtesy of Historic Photographs, Fine Arts Library, Harvard College Library.

Plate 6 Dharm Das (attrib.). Joint circumcision ceremony of the three sons of the Mughal Emperor, Akbar, performed on 22 October 1573, Mughal School, *c.* 1605, miniature painting, 23 × 12.5 cm, from a manuscript of the *Akbar-nama* of Abu'l-Fazl. Keir Collection, Richmond. Photo: A.C. Cooper, London.

Plate 7 Muhammad (attrib.). *A Young Woman with a White Veil*, Qajar, Persia, *c*. 1845, oil on canvas, 145 × 81 cm. Photo: Sotheby's Picture Library, London.

Plate 8 The Prophet with his Companions in a Mosque, page from a manuscript of the *Shahnama-i al-i Osman* (*Royal Book of the House of Osman*) of 'Arifi, Turkey, Istanbul, *c.* 1558, ink, opaque watercolour and gold on paper, 33.5 × 21 cm. Los Angeles County Museum of Art, The Nasli M. Heeramaneck Collection, gift of Joan Palevsky. Photo: © 2004 Museum Associates/LACMA.

Plate 9 The Prophet and his Companions and Associates bearing standards, early seventeenth century, miniature painting, 20 × 11 cm, one of thirteen miniatures from the *Siyer el-nebi*, the *Life of the Prophet* written by Mustafa ibn Yusuf Zarir of Erzurum in 1388. Keir Collection, Richmond. Photo: A.C. Cooper, London.

Plate 10 The Angel Gabriel revealing the Qur'an to the Prophet Muhammad. From Rashid al-Din, *History of the World*, Edinburgh University Special Collections.

being ascribed any special spiritual or hierarchical powers, and Ruthven argues that such decentralised religious authority tends to be conservative. However, perhaps this depends on other conditions. For example, we saw in studying Ruthven, Chapter 1, that decentralisation of authority from the '*ulama* to the newly literate and educated middle class, enabled by new communications technologies, has led to a new diversity of interpretations, ranging from the radical to the liberal.

2 Neoplatonism ascribes involvement with the material world to emanations from God rather than to God himself. God cannot be directly known, but only known through negation – knowledge of what he is not. This approach fits with the Islamic emphasis on God's utter transcendence and approach to affirmation through denial ('there is no god but God'), but adoption of Neoplatonist ideas into Islamic philosophy also led to a growing gap between the God of the Qur'an, who is described as acting in creation and sometimes described in anthropomorphic terms, and the remote, abstract God of the philosophers.

Neoplatonism also encouraged a rather elitist view of knowledge, in which the true meaning of texts was known only to an inner circle of initiates. This distinction between surface levels of understanding accessible to the masses and esoteric meanings available only to initiates prospered in Qur'anic interpretation under the Ismai'lis, who saw the imam as a source of special insight into the hidden meaning of the text. Important philosophers in the mainstream Sunni tradition – such as Ibn Sina (979–1037) and Ibd Rushd (1126–98) – were influenced by this Ismai'li way of thinking, although they were not formal members of the movement. Such 'differential hermeneutics' (i.e. the idea that different interpretations are appropriate to people at varying levels of understanding) are also evident in Sufism. □

EXERCISE

Ashura commemorates the martyrdom of Hussein, who Shi'ites believe was the rightful leader of the Muslim community. Hussein's martyrdom has come to symbolise the collective martyrdom of the Shi'ite people, who see themselves as having been forced to live as an often persecuted minority within the Sunni world for many centuries, a persecution continued in the modern era under some secular regimes. The footage on the DVD was shot by Iraqi journalist 'Salaam Pax' (an adopted name meaning 'peace' in Arabic and Latin) in 2004, when Shi'ites were free to celebrate the festival for the first time since the fall of Saddam Hussein in 2003. The first scenes were filmed in Baghdad, the rest in Karbala. The footage contains scenes of self-flagellation, which some viewers may find disturbing. Now view the 'Ashura' film on the DVD and consider the following questions:

1 Why was the commemoration of Ashura in 2004 a particularly important event for Shi'ite Muslims?

2 What context for understanding the scenes of self-flagellation does Salaam Pax suggest?

3 Can you think of parallels of self-mortification from other traditions which might shed light on this practice?

DISCUSSION

1 The commemoration of Ashura in 2004 is a particularly important event for Shi'ite Muslims because it was the first occasion in thirty years in which they could celebrate the festival without the restrictions imposed by Saddam Hussein's regime.

2 Salaam Pax stresses that some of what is witnessed may be over-exuberance in response to the lifting of restrictions. He indicates that some forms of self-flagellation are banned in Iran – an Islamic republic in which Shi'ism is the official religion – perhaps suggesting that in future, when exuberance at Saddam's departure has died down, the Iraqi authorities might wish to take similar action.

3 Self-mortification has its place in many, not least Christian, religious traditions. In Christianity it sometimes signifies a taming of humanity's baser nature; in Hinduism it may be a sign of the adept's self-mastery and spiritual development. But in Shi'ite Islam, the main emphasis is on the imitation of the suffering of Hussein, which is seen as redemptive. Probably the closest parallel to this is Christian identification with Christ's passion which, at times in Christian history and in some traditions, has involved partial re-enactments of the passion story entailing the suffering of participants. □

Sufism

Read Ruthven, 'Sufism' and 'Sufism and Shi'ism', pages 70 to 75, including the boxed texts.

EXERCISE

1 How do Sufi interpretations of Islam compare with those of the '*ulama* and Islamic philosophers?

2 How are Sufi and Shi'ite practices similar?

DISCUSSION

1 This question requires you to compare what you have learned so far about the *'ulama* and Islamic philosophers with your new reading in this section. The characteristic emphasis of Sufism is on the inward experience of God by the believer, stressing the reward of that experience in itself rather than any external effects (i.e. rewards or punishments). Various forms of *dhikr* ('remembrance' of God) are practised, involving meditative techniques such as recitation or chanting of the names of God, and bodily movements such as the ritualized spinning of the famous 'whirling dervishes' (see Ruthven, Figure 12 on page 132). The ultimate goal of such exercises is an experience of *fana*, which may be translated as 'annihilation of the individual in God'. The relationship with God is sometimes viewed as one of a lover, whereby the 'lover' experiences loss of self in total devotion to God as the loved one.

This interior and experiential emphasis contrasts with the 'Islam of the *'ulama*', which stresses conformity to the *shari'a*, and obedience to, rather than experience of, God. At times, Sufi practices developed in antinomian (anti-law) directions to the point of flouting *shari'a*, as with al-Hallaj's emphasis on 'internal' pilgrimage over the Qur'anically prescribed *hajj* to Mecca. The Sufi emphasis on experience and love of God also contrasts to some extent with the philosophers' God, which tended to be remote and abstract. However, these divergent tendencies in Islam can be seen as complementary or balancing one another. The *'ulama* provide guidance on Islam in everyday life to create the conditions in which spiritual development becomes possible; conversely the Sufis' inward development can create self-discipline for life's daily struggles. Similarly, the philosophical and Sufi emphases on God's transcendence and immanence respectively can be seen as balancing one another, creating a synthesis visible in the work of philosophers such as ibn 'Arabi.

2 Sufism and Shi'ism both see hidden, mystical meanings in the Qur'an, and look to special teachers – the Sufi 'friends' (of God) and Shi'ite imams, to reveal these meanings and some Sufi orders trace their lineage through 'Ali. There are, it is worth noting, some Shi'ite Sufi orders. ☐

Popular Sufism in South Asia

The following readings introduce several aspects of the Sufi tradition, and focus on one particular facet of it: the women who sing devotional songs at Sufi shrines across the Muslim world, from Morocco to India. As the first reading explains, Sufism has existed throughout Islamic history as a kind of counter tendency to the orthodoxy/orthopraxis (prescribed belief/practice) of the *'ulama*. Where the *'ulama* have emphasised the Arabic textual tradition and universal Islamic practice (such as the Five Pillars and *shari'a*), Sufism has used local languages, celebrated local holy people, and incorporated pre- and non-Islamic elements into its practice. The Sufi tradition is strong in South Asia, but also in most parts of the Muslim world, apart from the Wahhabi-dominated Saudi Arabia, and in other places and movements where Wahhabism has become influential. This is because Wahhabism, like a number of Islamic reform movements over the centuries, is hostile to Sufi practice, seeing *shirk* in its incorporation of local cultural and religious elements. Women have played (and continue to play) an important role in Sufi devotional practice, and Reading 9 introduces Reshma, a wandering gypsy woman who became famous singing at a Sufi shrine in Sind, Pakistan.

In introducing these female Sufi singers, the extracts confront the perception that women play a minimal role in Islamic worship, and therefore anticipate the topic of women in Islam that is the focus of Ruthven, Chapter 5. Read the following extract which is the Foreword to Shemeem Abbas's book, *The Female Voice in Sufi Ritual*. In it Elizabeth Warnock Fernea contextualises the study of women in Sufism and introduces the work and methods of Pakistani academic, Shemeen Abbas.

READING 9

The female voice in Sufi ritual

Western scholars have described Islam as a 'male' religion, a characterization that continues to be repeated well into the twenty-first century. As evidence for this position, commentators state and restate that no women are observed in the mosque for prayers, that only boys appear to be students in the Quranic schools, and that female participation is lacking during the major religious feasts (the Iid al Fitr which follows Ramadan, and the Iid al Adha, or feast of sacrifice). If this is actually the case, how could Islam be seen as other than male-focused? This view arises from several misconceptions.

Primary among these is the early scholars' need to compare Islam to a familiar system, i.e., Christianity. Such a comparison ignores a central fact: the mosque is not, like the Christian church, the center of religious observance. The focus of Muslim practice, like the focus of Judaic religious practice, lies in the home. The home is where the rituals marking the religious year take place and where women have tended to pray. And girls have always attended Quranic schools and received religious education, though often in private settings separate from boys. Further, early Western studies of Islam were text-based, rather than being the result of on-the-ground research and fieldwork in Muslim countries. The absence of a common language has also contributed to an ethnocentric view. Until very recently, knowledge of

Arabic, Persian, Turkish, Urdu, and other languages spoken by Muslims around the world was minimal in the West. Muslim scholars themselves only began to write in English, French, and German after the nineteenth-century incursions by Western colonial powers.

Ethnocentrism also affected scholars' recognition of the importance of different categories of religious behaviour that might not be present to the same degree in Christian practice. Here I speak of Sufism, or Islamic mysticism, and the far-flung series of lodges that the Sufi brotherhoods and sisterhoods have established over the centuries throughout the Islamic world. Sufi lodges, or *zawiyas*, are found from Morocco across the Fertile Crescent to Turkey, South Asia, and the Gulf States. (They are not found, of course, among Wahhabi adherents in Saudi Arabia.) Sufism, however, has always been regarded with some ambiguity by Muslim *imams* and *mullahs*, who see the rituals of the Sufi *tariqas* (organisations) as less than orthodox. But as is the case with all religious institutions, the way in which a belief is formally stated and the way in which it is expressed often differs among believers. Thus, just as the rise of holy figures and the pilgrimage to shrines such as Lourdes, Ste. Anne de Beaupré, and Our Lady of Guadalupe arouse controversies within the orthodox hierarchy of Christian Catholicism, so do the activities of the regional cults or organizations evoke mixed feelings among the theologians of Islam.

But the Sufi brotherhoods and sisterhoods have persisted, despite religious disfavor and government attempts to curtail their practices. In Libya, during the Italian colonial period it was the chain of Sufi Senussi lodges that kept Islamic learning alive and served as a rallying point for Muslims objecting to Italian occupation. Mustafa Kemal outlawed the Sufi lodges in the 1920s, believing that they had a deleterious influence on his country's modernization program, and also perhaps posed a political threat to his new republican government. In Morocco and Algeria, young survivors of the French colonial period saw the shrines as evidence of backwardness, and a program to discredit them began among the newly independent citizens. But the Sufi groups survived, and they continue to prosper throughout the Islamic world. Similar organizations are found in South Asia.

Sufi rituals vary from country to country and from rural to urban areas. In some, the lodge is an adjunct to the local mosque, and the activities are closely related. In others, the lodge is a separate building and organization. The organizations embrace both men and women in the rituals, sometimes separately, sometimes together in congregational settings. French ethnographers in North Africa noted early the *marabouts* (shrines) scattered through the countryside as well as the cities, shrines dedicated to *walis* (holy men), which are the focus of annual *moussems*, or celebrations of the lives of the holy men and women for whom the shrines are named. But the French ethnographers seldom mentioned the women auxiliaries of these same *marabouts*. It is only in the work of indigenous social scientists, such as the Tunisian anthropologist Sophie Ferchiou, that we find accounts of women's participation in annual rituals, and their daily or monthly visits (*ziarat*) to the shrines. And almost nothing has been published in English about men and women in South Asian Sufism.

Given these gaps in Western scholarships about Islam, then, it is a great pleasure to introduce the book that follows: *The Female Voice in Sufi Ritual*, by Shemeem Abbas. Dr. Abbas is a native of Pakistan who has lived and studied in the West over a period of several years and holds advanced degrees from both British and American universities. Dr. Abbas' first interest in South Asian Sufis focused on the linguistic and performance aspects of their regular rituals. For her doctoral dissertation, she documented performances and linguistic variations within Pakistani communities. She attended sessions not only in her native land, but also England and the United States, where Pakistanis far from home were developing their own versions of traditional rituals.

Now Dr. Abbas has built upon her earlier research to give us the following work. She has set down events in the ritual cycle in which both men and women are participants. Through her work in historical archives, she has discovered early examples of women's roles as participants, performers, and creators of texts. In travels throughout Pakistan, she visited village and city groups, recorded local variants of rituals, and interviewed not only the Sufi singers (both men and women), but also members of the audiences and local critics. This was possible because of her command of local languages, which allowed her access to local oral traditions. She has translated many of the texts in a fluid and accessible style. Dr. Abbas' research and insight has allowed her to integrate this new material into a South Asian case study, an in-depth view, in English, of women's role in Sufism.

The Female Voice in Sufi Ritual will come as no surprise to Muslim readers. But for Western audiences, it offers an introduction to an area of religious expression – that of women – which has been largely ignored and which is important to all people in the diverse world of Islam.

Source: Shemeem Abbas, The Female Voice in Sufi Ritual *(Austin, TX: University of Texas Press, 2002), xiii–xv.*

EXERCISE

Having read the 'Foreword' by Elizabeth Warnock Fernea, answer the following questions:

1 Why has Western scholarship under-estimated the role of women in Muslim worship?

2 How is Sufism organised?

3 What methods did Abbas use to research *The Female Voice in Sufi Ritual*?

DISCUSSION

1 Western scholarship has tended to under-estimate the role of women in Muslim worship for several reasons: first, because it has approached Islam using the model of Christianity, it has focused on the mosque as analogue for the church to the neglect of the network of Sufi lodges, and on formal congregational worship to the neglect of domestic and informal worship; secondly, it has tended to be text-based, and hence to neglect practices not reflected in texts; thirdly, Western study has been limited because much religious practice involving women takes place in local languages, which have not been well known in the West.

2 Sufism is organised in *tariqas* (organisations), both for men and women (brotherhoods and sisterhoods), which meet in lodges (*zawiyas*). Local shrines (*marabouts*) to holy men and women, annual festivities to celebrate them (*moussems*), living holy men (called *walis* in Morocco, *pirs* in South Asia), and often female women attendants at these shrines, play important roles. Relationships to local mosques and religious establishments vary from the complementary to the antagonistic.

3 Abbas researched the role of women in ritual at or around Sufi shrines by examining the language of the songs sung by the women, the way they are performed, and by interviewing the women themselves, audience members and local critics, both in Pakistan and diaspora communities in the US and UK. □

Now read the following section by Abbas herself:

READING 9 CONTINUED

History and economy of women in Sufi ritual

The great religious and spiritual renaissance in India that started around the fourteenth century reached its peak under the Mughal emperor Akbar in the sixteenth century. He patronized the fusion of Sufi mystical Islam with the indigenous practices of the subcontinent, and he himself was an ardent devotee of Shaikh Saleem Chishti, a Sufi mystic who, according to legend, prayed for him so that he would have a son. His prayers were answered when Saleem, later known as Jehangir, was born and succeeded Akbar to the Mughal throne.

Thus the mystic poetry of India, including that of Sufism in the fourteenth and fifteenth centuries, was emotional and expressed the devotees' love towards a personal God. The movements that emerged at this time challenged hegemonic religious authority, caste boundaries, gender inequity, and the exclusive use of elitist language in religion.[10] In South Asian Islam, the trend appeared in Sufism and particularly in the *sufiana-kalam* traditions that used poetry written in the vernaculars by the Sufi poets. As stated earlier, since this model was an indigenous one that required minimal musical skills and resources, women's input in the singing of this poetry is visible. Mira Bai, the Rajput princess who 'disappeared' among the people and whose *bhajans* (devotional poems) are sung among the minstrels in India, is a telling example of the roving-minstrel tradition.

Since the *sufiana-kalam* tradition of singing mystical texts in the vernaculars was based on the roving-minstrel culture, there are indigenous devotional elements in them. In this form of worship the emphasis is on the repetition of God's name.[11]

In the Sind region Shah Abdul Latif (d. 1752 AD) and other Sufi poets composed poetry in the vernacular languages and dialects in which they sang as roving mendicants within an Islamic framework. For fear of the clergy mystic poetry sung to music remained confined to the minstrel class.[12] That is why the *sufiana-kalam* traditions are strong among this class of roving musicians who sing in the indigenous languages such as Siraiki, Sindhi, Baluchi, and the regional dialects of Pakistan. This further explains why the non-Muslim Kolhi and Bhil communities are devotees of Shah Abdul Latif's shrine in Bhit Shah, Sind: his poetry is linguistically diverse and is tolerant of other beliefs.

The Sufi mystical traditions came to the subcontinent of Pakistan and India through the Sind province with the coming of Islam in 708 AD when Muhammad bin Qasim conquered the region. Muhammad bin Qasim was an Arab general of the Ommayad dynasty who came to

[10] Encyclopedia Britannica website, 'Bhakti Movement of Medieval India.' Additionally, see Saiyid Athar Abbas Rizvi, 'The interaction between medieval Hindu mystic traditions and Sufism', in *A History of Sufism in India*, vol. I, 322–96.

[11] *Ibid.*

[12] Tirathdas Hotechand, 'The *Risalo*: its musical compositions', in *Shah Abdul Latif: His Mystical Poetry*, ed. Abdul Hamid Akhund (Hyderabad: Shah Abdul Latif Bhit Shah Cultural Center Committee, 1991), 162.

Sind through the land route from Iran. After his conquest, a long line of Sufi mystics came to the region through Baluchistan, Mekran, Multan, and Sind itself. In the province of Sind alone there are said to be more than a hundred thousand Sufi shrines. Sufi mystics additionally came through the northern routes to the subcontinent. They came from Arabia, Iran, Iraq, Turkey, Afghanistan, and the entire region that is now the Middle East and the Central Asian Republics.

The Sufi version of Islam in Pakistan and India was based on syncretism and reconciled differing beliefs. It was holistic as it blended in with the beliefs of local cultures and populations who were Dravidians, Aryans, Hindus, Buddhists, and all native creeds. At that time in India many converted to Islam because it offered relief from the caste oppression. Thus, through Sufism, an indigenous model of Islam evolved in the subcontinent. Since some of these cultures were 'matrimythical'[13] and used the indigenous female myths, the Sufi poets creatively blended the female voices from these myths into their poetry that they sang to music. The purpose was mainly aesthetic and devotional.

[...]

Reshma and Mast Qalandar

In this section I explore some aspect of the personal histories of women musicians who sing devotional Sufi poetry. Their histories, told partly by themselves and partly by others, show how the melodies that they sang at Sufi shrines became the marks of their personal identities. I present some performative contexts.

During my fieldwork in Sind at the Hazrat Lal Shahbaz Qalandar shrine in 1999, I studied women roving minstrels who sing devotional narratives to the Sufi saints. I looked for them at this shrine because Reshma, who was once a roving gypsy woman, rose to international fame while she sang her famous 'Mast Qalandar' melody here in the late sixties. Women informants who live around the heavily populated area of the shrine reported that during the '*urs* celebrations, which last for more than a week, it is almost impossible to walk in the narrow streets of the city. Sehwan, the historic city built within a large fortress from the time of Alexander the Great, is flooded with large numbers of female musicians who converge on the city to earn a living. The informants reported that most of the women musicians come from the

[13] This is a term created by Jacqueline Henkel of the Department of English at the University of Texas at Austin.

Panjab and the neighbourhoods of Sind itself. They perform in every nook and cranny and attract huge audiences.

I found that a favourite melody, sung in the roving-minstrel tradition, is the 'Mast Qalandar' *dhun*, a tune reported to be sung all along the Rajasthan, Sind, Baluchistan, and Iran continuum. Reshma sang it in Siraiki at the Lal Shahbaz Qalandar shrine in the sixties with a passion that made her internationally renowned. The melody is dedicated to 'Ali and is sung in all the regional languages along the continuum. Almost every folksinger in the region can sing it because of its simple mnemonics and rhythm. The lyric, although dedicated to 'Ali, is also dedicated to Hazrat Lal Shahbaz Qalandar, a Sifi mystic of Sind. Hazrat Lal Shahbaz is venerated in the lyric as the bestower of children.[14] Reshma's performance uses the standard lyric sung in the popular 'Mast Qalandar' folk melody:

Lal meri pat rakio bhala	O Lal Qalandar, save my prestige
Jhole Lalan	O thou of the cradle
Sindhri da	O thou of Sind
Sehwan da	Of Sehwan
Sakhi Shahbaz Qalandar	Thou bounteous Shahbaz Qalandar
Dama dam mast Qalandar	Thy ecstatic trance is the healing breath
Ali Shahbaz Qalandar	O 'Ali-Shahbaz Qalandar
Ali dam dam de andar	'Ali's name is the healing breath
Ma va nu pira bachre dena	Thou giver of children to mothers
Behna nu dena-e vir bhala	Thou giver of brothers to sisters
Jhule Lalan	O thou of the cradle
Sindhri da	O thou of Sind
Sehwan da	Of Sehwan
Sakhi Shahbaz Qalandar	Thou bounteous Shahbaz Qalandar
Ali dam dam de andar	'Ali's name is the healing breath

Performers like Reshma sing the melody in their high-pitched, full-throated voices at the shrine without the support of microphones. They also sing poetic texts that glorify the *karamat* (mystical prowess) of Hazrat Lal Shahbaz Qalandar. The Sufi saint is known as a *jalali pir*, a mystic with intense supernatural energy.

[14] I have discussed the melody with both Muslim and non-Muslim informants and conclude that there is no fixed interpretation. The lyric is drawn cross culturally from the regional folklore.

The female roving minstrels are accompanied by small groups of instrumentalists perhaps playing percussion or accordion. But, by and large, they have minimal instruments. They will either play a *yak-tara* or a *ghara*, an earthen pot used as a drum. Their identity is a ring (*chala*), which they wear around the middle finger and use to create percussion on a *lota*, (aluminum pot) or a *ghara*. These minstrels are called *lotevali* for playing the *lota*, *chalevali* for playing the *chala*, or *gharevali* for playing the *ghara*.[15]

The *lotevali* or *chalevali* are roving gypsy women who move from one shrine to another while their families trade in livestock and peddle inexpensive local textiles and pots and pans. Their audiences are women and men from their own socioeconomic background who participate in the shrine activities at the time of the *'urs* and who give them small sums of money during the performance. Women tend to pay less because they are unemployed, while men can be more generous.

Source: Shemeem Abbas, The Female Voice in Sufi Ritual *(Austin, TX: University of Texas Press, 2002), 18–19, 25–7.*

EXERCISE

Listen to the recording of Reshma singing 'Mast Qalandar' on Audio CD 1, track 30.

Consider the following questions, reflecting on Reading 9 and Reshma's music:

1 What are your responses to hearing Reshma's music? Was it what you had expected after reading about it? What emotions and associations did it evoke?

2 What was characteristic of the mystical poetry of India in the sixteenth century, and how did this tradition feed into Sufi poetry and song?

3 What are the characteristics of the 'Mast Qalandar' song performed by Reshma, and in what contexts is the song performed?

DISCUSSION

1 This exercise is a good opportunity for you to discuss your reactions with other students. You might like to do this via the student forum, or at your next tutorial.

2 This poetry was emotional and expressed the devotees' love towards a personal God. It was often sung by wandering female minstrels

[15] They additionally sing around shrines in Multan and Sahiwal to earn a living.

(just as in the Hindu *bhakti* (devotional) tradition). This form of poetry influenced the Sufi tradition, which had been present in the Sind region since the early eighth century. Sufi poets such as Shah Abdul Latif (eighteenth century) blended female voices in this devotional tradition into Sufi poetry and song, which remained mostly in local languages to avoid conflict with the 'clergy' (*'ulama*).

3 'Mast Qalandar' ('intoxicated dervish' – dervish being a Sufi devotee) is a devotional song dedicated to 'Ali (Muhammad's cousin) and Hazrat Lal Shahbaz Qalandar, a local Sind Sufi saint. Its simple melody means that it can be widely sung in local languages by folksingers from Rajasthan (north-west India) in the east to Iran in the West. It reveres the healing properties of 'Ali, the fertility-giving properties attributed to the dervish, and refers to ecstatic trance of the Sufi mystic. □

EXERCISE

Now view the 'Sufi Shrine: Hazrat Nizamuddin Shrine, Delhi' film on the DVD and consider the following questions:

1 What do those interviewed see as the most important aspects of Sufi tradition?

2 Why do Sikhs and Muslims also worship at this Sufi shrine? What might be significant about the sharing of food among people of different faiths in an Indian context?

3 What does the notice (written in English) on the entrance to the tomb say? What does this suggest about the emphasis on universality among those interviewed, and the stress on the important role of women in Sufi tradition in Ruthven (2012) and this study guide?

DISCUSSION

1 They emphasise the direct link between the believer and God, the place of charity as a way of pleasing God, and the role of music in worship.

2 The Hindu interviewee, Hari Babu, says that he learned at the shrine that religious differences are not important: 'all differences end here'. The Sikh interviewee, Pritpal Singh Johar, describes the shrine as a place where he feels part of a 'universal family'. In the Hindu caste system, there are strict rules about who can receive food from whom, and hence restrictions on who can eat together. Muslims, Hindus and Sikhs all eating together (in this case, feasting after the Muslim fast of Ramadan) may be seen as challenging this form of social taboo. The Sikh faith also challenges this taboo, offering food to all visitors to a Gurdwara (Sikh temple).

3 If you look carefully, you will see that there is a notice on the outside of the tomb forbidding entry to women. You will also notice that men and women sit separately to eat and worship. This suggests that although Sufism allows women a role in worship (e.g. by singing devotional songs at shrines), nonetheless (at least in this South Asian context) it follows local cultural norms by maintaining social distinctions between the genders, and by upholding some kind of taboo against women as in some way polluted, by not allowing them entry to the most sacred places. □

Shi'ism and Iran

Read Ruthven, 'Shi'ism and Iran', on pages 75 to 81.

EXERCISE

How does the role of the Shi'ite *'ulama* differ from that of the Sunnis, and how did political and other developments in the last 200 years pave the way for Ayatollah Khomeini's concept of *Vilayet-e faqih* ('rule of the expert in Islamic law') to become popular in Iran by 1979?

DISCUSSION

The Shi'ite *'ulama* have had more authority to develop *shari'a* than the Sunnis. Whereas Sunnis have been largely bound to *taqlid* (imitation) of precedent, Shi'ite clergy have exercised the right to new interpretation (*ijtihad*) throughout their history. In addition, their powers of new interpretation have been enhanced by their role as deputies of the Hidden Imam.

The location of several centres of Shi'ite learning (e.g. Karbala and Najaf in Iraq) outside the main area of Shi'ite political power (Persia, later Iran) worked to the advantage of the Shi'ite clergy. Their independence was encouraged by the rulers of adjacent territories (Ottoman, then Iraqi), for whom they served to undermine the authority of the leaders (Persian, then Iranian) across the border. Furthermore, within Persia/Iran the clergy's landownership and receipt of income from shrines put them in a strong position to challenge the ruling authorities.

These factors worked in favour of Ayatollah Khomeini in the events leading up to his successful coup in 1979. Granted political asylum in the Iraqi city of Najaf in 1963, he developed his theory of the 'rule of the expert in Islamic law' (*Vilayet-e faqih*), which argued that, following the activist precedent of 'Ali's son Hussein, the *'ulama* have the right to seize power in the event of a corrupt regime.

Additional elements which also worked in Khomeini's favour were the American intervention in the region, and the presence of new communications technologies. In the case of the former, in the interests of rapprochement between Iraq and Iran the Americans persuaded Saddam Hussein to expel Khomeini, who fled to Paris. But this, in fact, gave him better access to the world's press and communications systems, so that he was able to raise his international profile as a potential alternative to the corrupt Shah, and to disseminate materials (tapes and photocopies of sermons) through sympathetic networks in Iran to a mass audience. Thus by 1979 he was in a strong enough position both within Iran and internationally to return from exile to Iran in triumph (see Ruthven, 2012, 79). □

Islamic unity and diversity in architectural practice: the mosque

In the context of Ruthven, Chapter 3, on unity and diversity, we will now examine the common features and regional diversity of mosques. The basic function of the mosque is as a place for the performance of *salat*, the prayer ritual which Muslims are expected to perform individually five times a day, and collectively (especially for men) at least at Friday noon (*juma*) prayers. Hence the basic requirements of a mosque are quite straightforward – a space with an indication for the direction of prayer (*mihrab*) towards the Ka'ba at Mecca. Thus the prayer space laid out for private use for guests in a Pakistani hotel in Figure 3 satisfies the basic requirements for a mosque.

Figure 3 Prayer space for Pakistani hotel guests. Photo: © Hasan Uddin-Khan.

However, other widespread features have developed, and Figure 4 shows the common standard components of a mosque. These include a *minbar* or pulpit (always situated to the right of the *mihrab)* from which the address or sermon (*khutba*) is preached after Friday prayers (see the *mihrab* in Figure 5); the *kursi*, a lectern from which the Qur'an is recited; and the *dikka*, a raised platform on which the words and actions of the prayer can be demonstrated. Externally, a courtyard containing a fountain for the ritual washing (*wudu*) required prior to prayer, and a minaret (a tower from which the call to prayer can be issued) have become common features.

Around these widely shared features, a large array of regional forms gradually developed, as Figure 6 demonstrates. These sketches illustrate seven distinctive regional styles, from the Arabian heartland model, with its single courtyard and covered area most closely resembling the standard style described, to the Chinese style, with its walled garden and detached pavilions, the Anatolian or Ottoman style, with its distinctive high minarets and massive central dome (the latter inspired by St Sofia, the great imperial Christian church constructed in Constantinople, later converted into a mosque in present-day Istanbul), and the distinctive mud-brick style of the sub-Saharan West African mosque. Mosques also vary greatly according to size, from intimate to truly massive, and in terms of level of decoration, from plain to elaborate.

EXERCISE

As you look at the following photographs in Figures 7 to 14, which, if any, of the regional styles of mosque, shown in Figure 6, do they illustrate? Which typical feature can you pick out?

DISCUSSION

Figure 7 is in the Chinese style. The feature shown is The Tower of Introspection, a minaret from The Great Mosque in Xian. Islam spread to China as early as the eighth century CE, and this mosque dates from 792 CE.

Figure 8 is in the sub-Saharan West African style. This mosque is also the tomb of a Sufi saint, Askia Muhammad, in Gao, Mali. The picture shows the tower/minaret with external ramps and steps, and was rebuilt in its present form in the nineteenth century. (You can see another example of architecture from Mali in Ruthven, Figure 10, on page 129.)

Figure 9 is in the Iran (Persian)/Central Asian style. This can be deduced from the multiple courtyards and domes. This mosque is in Isfahan in Iran, as is the mosque shown in Plate 5.

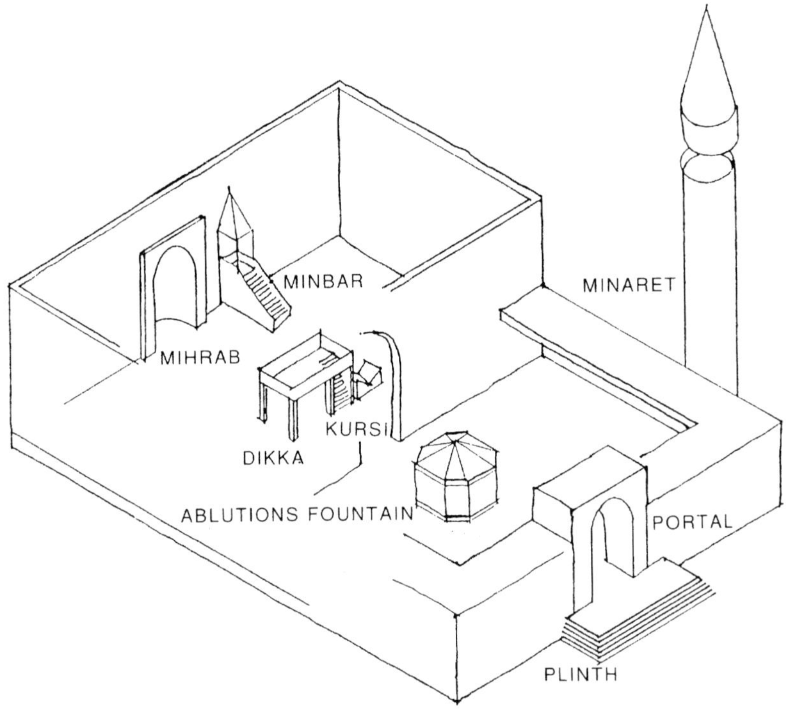

The standard components of the mosque (not drawn to scale or representing any individual mosque).

Figure 4 Standard components of the mosque (line diagram), sketch by Martin Frishman. From M. Frishman and H. Khan, *The Mosque, History, Architectural Development and Regional Diversity*, Thames and Hudson, 1994.

Figure 10 is in the South-East Asian style. Although the central tower and upper roof lines are ornate, this mosque at Lubuk Bauk, West Sumatra (Indonesia), with its predominantly triangular roofs, most closely fits the South-East Asian style. The roofs, now corrugated iron, were originally thatched.

The modern mosque in Figure 11 does not fit with any traditional regional style. Built in the socialist period in Bosnia (then part of the republic of Yugoslavia, 1948–93), the architect of Sherefudin's White Mosque in Visoko rejected the traditional Ottoman heritage of the region in favour of a modernist style.

Figure 12 is the Central London Mosque, Regent's Park, London. Built by Sir Frederick Gibberd and Partners, a firm of English architects, in 1977, this mosque reflects an eclectic range of regional styles: although it is a single tower, the tall minaret is reminiscent of the Ottoman style; the

Figure 5 Mihrab of the Mosque-Madrassa of al-Muayyad Shaykh, Cairo, 1415–22. Courtesy of the Fine Arts Library, Harvard College Library.

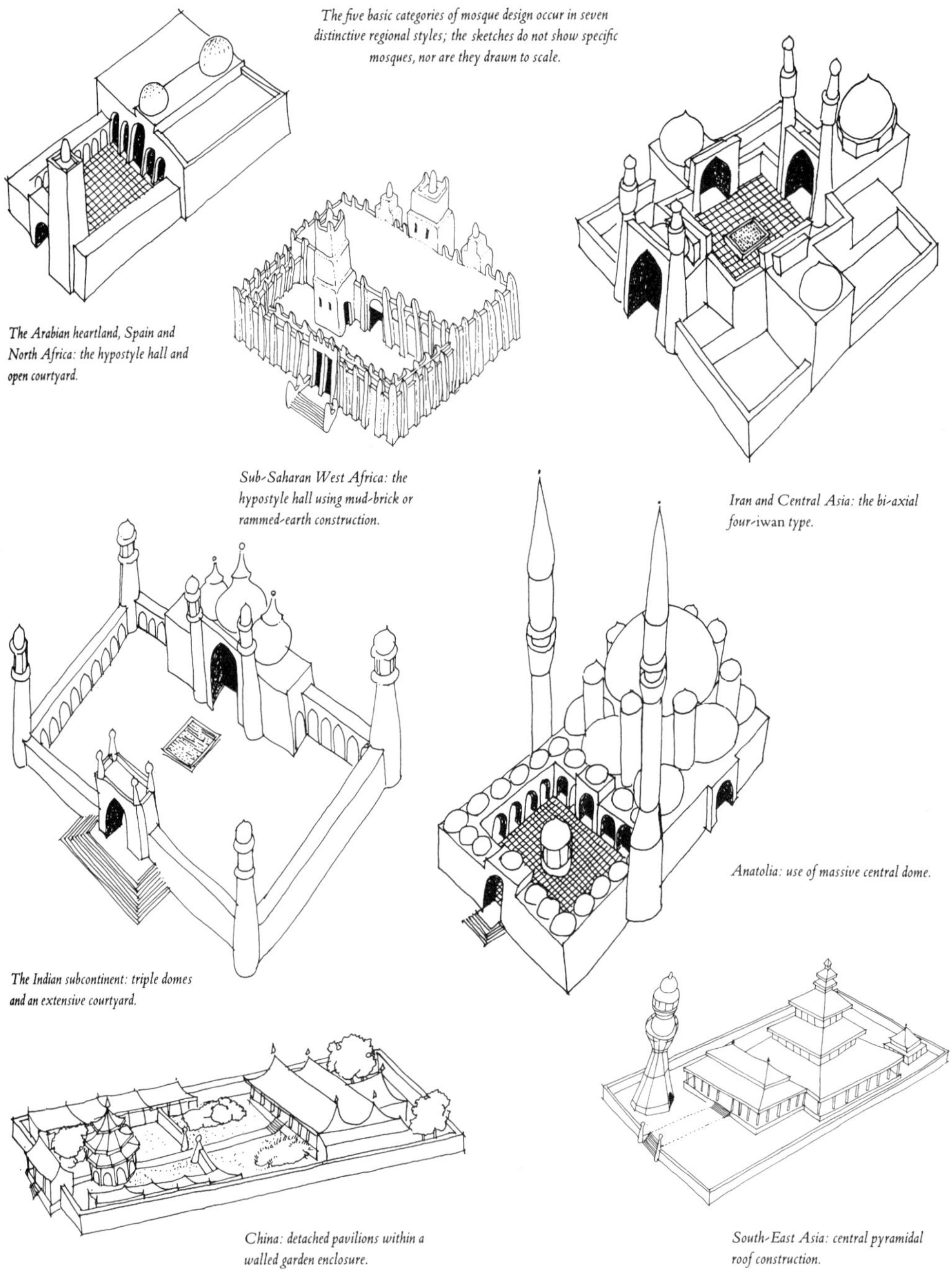

Figure 6 The five basic categories of mosque design in seven regional styles (seven line diagrams), sketched by Martin Frishman. From M. Frishman and H. Khan, *The Mosque, History, Architectural Development and Regional Diversity*, Thames and Hudson, 1994.

Figure 7 Bangke Tower of Introspection, the Great Mosque of Xi'an, China, 1984. Photo: Cherie Wendelken and You-Huan Zhu, Courtesy of the Aga Khan Visual Archive, M.I.T.

Figure 8 Mosque-mausoleum of Askia Muhammad, Gao, Mali, view of the tower-minaret with external ramps and stairs (rebuilt in its present form in the nineteenth century). Photo: Archives La Documentation française; Photo Gouvernement général AOF.

Figure 9 Friday Mosque, Isfahan, aerial view. © Roland and Sabrina Michaud. Photo: NB Pictures.

metal plating of the dome is reminiscent of some Indian mosques, but also resembles the distinctive Dome of the Rock, Jerusalem. You may also find the shape of the dome reminiscent of the Masjid-i Shah, Isfahan, shown in Plate 5.

The modern mosque shown in Figure 13, dating from the 1980s, has multiple minarets in the Ottoman style, while the triangular roofs are reminiscent of the South-East Asian style. It is situated in Islamabad, Pakistan, and demonstrates how the fusion of styles in a globalising world is not restricted to the Muslim diaspora, but is also a feature of the Muslim-majority world.

The prefabricated 'instant domes' in Figure 14 are in the Indian style (onion shaped), but on sale by the roadside in Indonesia. Prefabricated building techniques and a resurgence of private mosques across much of the Muslim-majority world has brought in the 'age of the DIY mosque'. □

Figure 10 Mosque at Lubuk Bauk, West Sumatra, Indonesia. Photo: © Hugh O'Neill.

Figure 11 Sherefudin's White Mosque, Visoko, Bosnia, 1983. Photo: Jacques Betant, Courtesy of the Aga Khan Visual Archive, M.I.T.

Figure 12 Central London Mosque at Regent's Park, London, 1965. Photo: Getty Images.

Figure 13 The Shah (King) Faisal Mosque, Islamabad, 1985. Courtesy of Vedat Dalgkay/Aga Khan Trust for Culture, Geneva.

Figure 14 Prefabricated 'instant domes', for sale at the roadside in Indonesia. Photo: © Suha Özkan.

EXERCISE

On the DVD, architectural historian Ratish Nanda describes the features of the Jama Masjid Mosque in Delhi, the largest mosque in India. He explains the development of mosque architecture in India, and explains how mosque architecture across the world draws on and incorporates elements of local culture. Now view this part of the DVD and consider the following questions:

1 How did mosque architecture in India develop, how does the Jama Masjid illustrate the influence of Shah Jahan, and when was it built?

2 How has mosque architecture related to local culture, and in what ways does the Jama Masjid illustrate this trend?

DISCUSSION

1 In India from the 1400s, mosques evolved from being covered to featuring a large courtyard. Shah Jahan placed a particular emphasis on symmetry, and the Jama Masjid shows his influence by being constructed symmetrically around a central axis. Shah Jahan developed the cusped arch and fluted column, which feature in the Jama Masjid. The mosque was built in the mid-seventeenth century.

2 Mosque architecture has tended to incorporate elements of local culture, adapting it to reflect Islamic beliefs. Islamic teaching restricts the representation of animals and people because of the danger of *shirk* (idolatry), but in the Jama Masjid, Indian styles and techniques of representation are used to produce geometric and floral designs, displaying the lotus bud in particular. □

Geographical diversity in Islam

This section of the study guide has introduced some of the historical causes of diversity in Islam, and examined some of the cultural manifestations of that diversity as expressed in the Sufi tradition and in mosque architecture around the world. The following short exercise directs you to Map 1 in Ruthven (2012, xv) to consider some of the geographical diversity of Islam. It will be useful to have an atlas in front of you for this exercise, as the map marks the boundaries but not names of contemporary nations.

EXERCISE

Question: how are Muslims distributed around the world?

DISCUSSION

The areas with the highest proportions of Muslim settlement lie in a continuous band of land from Pakistan in the east to Morocco in the West, then in Bangladesh, and in South-East Asia (Malaysia and Indonesia). However, most areas of the world have at least a small Muslim population (2 to 5 per cent). In addition, given the concentration on Middle Eastern Islam in the media, it is worth noting that the countries with the largest Muslim populations are in fact, Indonesia (*c*. 205 million) and Pakistan and India (both *c*. 180 million). □

This section has reflected on different aspects of the themes of unity and diversity in Islam: theologically, historically, architecturally, geographically, and in terms of worship. The next section focuses on *sharī'a*, a core aspect of Islamic identity and practice.

8
Shari'a and its consequences

Popular portrayals of *shari'a* often focus on the penalties associated with it – such as the stoning of adulterers, amputation of hands for theft, or beheading of murderers. This section of the study guide aims to get behind these sensationalist images to understand the meaning and place of *shari'a* in Islamic faith and practice.

Read Ruthven, Chapter 4, 'Introduction', on pages 82 to 84.

EXERCISE

1 What did *shari'a* originally mean, and why has it become so important in Muslim societies?

2 How did *shari'a* develop during the first three centuries of Islam?

DISCUSSION

1 *Shari'a* originally meant 'the way to a watering place', with associations in the Qur'an of a path to both earthly and heavenly nourishment. Ruthven suggests that part of the reason for *shari'a*'s prominence in Muslim societies is the lack of a distinct sacred institution – like the Church in Christianity – to convey Islamic teaching. The argument here is that in the absence of such an institution to explain, nurture and enforce religious behaviour, fuller codification of religious rules is required. Another reason is that *shari'a* encompasses a broad range of human action – not just law in the limited Western sense, but also ritual, habits and customs.

2 During the period of the first four caliphs, legal rulings were based on the Qur'an, local customs, and the authority of the caliphs themselves, who clearly saw themselves as having some of the Prophet's divine authority. Thus, for example, the caliph 'Umar increased the penalty for *zina* (illicit sex) from the hundred lashes stated in the Qur'an to stoning to death. However, the struggles for leadership of the Islamic community, the challenges from the Shi'ites, and the unpopularity of caliphal attempts to impose a religious orthodoxy all undermined the authority of the caliphate, and gradually only the actions and words of the Prophet and the Qur'an came to be regarded as legitimate substantive sources of *shari'a* – although some changes made by the caliphs have remained, such as 'Umar's ruling on the penalty for adultery. ☐

The other two valid sources of law concern processes used for reaching a decision – *ijma‘* (consensus) and *qiyas* (reasoning by analogy). The next section considers the four traditionally recognised sources (*usul*) – the Qur'an, *hadith*, *ijma‘* and *qiyas* – in more depth.

Sources of *shari‘a*

Read Ruthven, 'The roots of Islamic law', pages 84 to 89, including the boxed texts.

EXERCISE

1 Taking each source in turn, what guidance does it provide, and what room for ambiguity or disagreement does it leave?

2 What are the five schools of Islamic law?

DISCUSSION

1 Characteristics of the four sources of *shari‘a* are:

(a) The Qur'an is the first and prime source of Islamic law, and contains a number of passages – mostly from the Medinese period – which include various rules and legal principles. These concern: diet; family; inheritance and marriage law (including inheritance rights for women); the *hudud* (singular *hadd*) punishments for armed robbery, sex outside marriage, slander, wine-drinking and apostasy; commercial transactions such as rules on contracts and the banning of *riba* (lending money at interest); and evidence (e.g. witnesses). But only about 10 per cent of the Qur'an contains legal material, and there are many areas of law not touched on, which leaves much room for debate. Furthermore, some verses appear to contradict each other, so decisions need to be taken as to which is given priority (in general, the later verses supersede the earlier ones).

(b) *Sunna*, the example of the Prophet as recorded in the *hadiths*, is the second source. This contains a good deal more detailed material than the Qur'an, but there are debates internal to the Muslim tradition about the reliability of some of this material, and there is also the issue of some contradictory traditions.

(c) The idea of *ijma‘* ('consensus') stems from the Prophet's saying 'my community will never agree upon an error'. Discussion over the years has concerned the scope of those to be included in the debate leading to consensus. Muslim tradition came to argue that when the community was small, consensus could reasonably be arrived at on a broad basis; but as Islam spread, the need to tie the diversifying community more closely to the Qur'an and Prophetic precedent grew, so consensus came to be interpreted as that of the *'ulama* who were in a position to judge opinions in relation to these traditions. However, since the nineteenth century, modernists and later Islamists have argued that *ijma'* should be extended again to whole communities, in line with mass education and democratic norms. In general, the requirement for consensus exercises a conservative effect on law-making, but provides no particular guidance.

(d) *Qiyas* provides a way to extend the scope of the precedents contained in the Qur'an and *sunna*, so that they may include situations and behaviours which resemble those found in these sources. However, as the example of the Qur'anic prohibition of wine drinking shows, this is far from straightforward. Some jurists have argued that the reason wine is forbidden is because of its intoxicating properties, and through *qiyas* have extended the ban to include other intoxicants. Liberal commentators might argue that if intoxication is the issue, then moderate consumption of wine should not be a problem. It has also been argued that since wine is explicitly prohibited in the Qur'an, its consumption is entirely forbidden, but other intoxicants may be consumed in moderation because they have not been specifically mentioned. Clearly, although guidance is thus extended, this is an inherently controversial process.

2 The four Sunni schools are Shafi'i, Hanafi, Maliki and Hanbali. The Shi'ite school is the Ja'fari, which in addition to the Sunni sources also includes *hadiths* of 'Ali and the imams alongside those of the Prophet. The Hanbali school tends to be the most conservative, the Hanafi the most liberal (and widespread). □

New interpretation and the holistic character of *shari'a*

Read Ruthven, '*Ijtihad*: the struggle for truth' and 'The Shari'a: an all-encompassing ideal', pages 89 to 94, including the boxed texts.

EXERCISE

1 What is *ijtihad*, and how important has its exercise been in the development of *shari'a*?

2 What are the five categories according to which the classical law books of Islam classified human behaviour, and how have *shari'a* courts been complemented in practice in Muslim history?

DISCUSSION

1 *Ijtihad* comes from the same root as *jihad*, meaning 'struggle', and is usually translated as 'effort' or, in the context of interpreting *shari'a*, as 'new interpretation'. It refers to the independent reasoning necessary to discern *shari'a* in new or changing circumstances. *Ijtihad* was important in the early centuries of Islam, but diminished in the Sunni law schools in the tenth and eleventh centuries. The doctrine of the closing of the 'gates of *ijtihad*' developed to justify this conservatism, but in spite of this it did not cease until at least the sixteenth century (except for the Hanbalis). Since the nineteenth century, first modernists and then Islamists have called for the re-opening of the gates of *ijtihad*, so its importance has greatly increased again in the modern period. In Shi'ite Islam it never ceased, and as we saw in Ruthven, Chapter 4, the pace of change quickened in the twentieth century.

2 These are *wajib/fard* (obligatory), *haram/mahzur* (forbidden), *mandub, masnun, mustahhab, sunna* (recommended); *makruh* (discouraged); and *jaiz, mubah* (neutral). They thus cover the whole range of human behaviour, not just behaviour that would normally be regulated by law in the Western sense.

Over time *shari'a* courts came to be supplemented by other specialised legal institutions, such as police courts dealing with criminal matters, the Inspector of Markets (*muhtasib*) dealing with commercial regulation, and caliphal courts dealing with legislation introduced by the caliph. Later, under European colonial influence, the powers of the *shari'a* courts were further eroded by the introduction of European systems based on Roman and common law practices. □

Shari'a and society

Read Ruthven, 'The Shari'a and Muslim societies', on pages 94 to 99, including boxed texts.

EXERCISE

1 What characterises the kind of justice administered by the *qadi* (judge) in a *shari'a* court, according to the quotations from Rosen in the boxed texts?

2 How has the *shari'a* influenced the development of institutions in Muslim societies over the centuries?

DISCUSSION

1 The justice administered by the *qadi* is aimed at putting people in a position where they are able to negotiate their own allowable (as established by God) relationships, rather than at bringing them into line with some higher authority (whether the state or God). However, this kind of jurisdiction has been increasingly eroded by the growth of the state in the modern period, which takes an increasing interest in closely regulating the lives of its citizens.

2 The emphasis on correct practice rather than belief has meant that Islam has left a deep imprint on the daily life of Muslim societies, and the *shari'a* has been the main vehicle for this. Although women were protected under the *shari'a*, it also institutionalised gender inequalities, and rules on inheritance and forbidding the charging of interest on loaned money prevented the accumulation of capital which arguably limited commercial activity. The construction of society in terms of individual relationships prevented the development of corporate entities and a public sphere, which (again arguably) may have restricted the development of commerce and of democratic politics. □

While Ruthven is careful not to say that corruption in modern Muslim-majority societies has to do with Islam (2012, 97), he does nonetheless imply that the economic and political development of Muslim societies has been restricted by the influence of *shari'a*. This is a controversial claim, and has been challenged by other scholars. For example, Therborn (1997) argues that, in spite of some legal differences, at least some Muslim urban centres developed complex and vibrant associational life of the kind which led eventually to the formation of democratic politics in Europe. Democracy did not develop internally in Muslim societies more because of the experience of colonial domination at a crucial stage of development, rather than because of fundamental differences in social structure caused by *shari'a*. However, this remains a hotly disputed topic.

Colonisation was also arguably a critical factor in shaping Muslim attitudes to women in the modern period, and it is to this contentious subject that we now turn.

9
Women, family and gender issues

Probably no set of issues is more controversial in the study of Islam than those surrounding women. However, the debates are far from straightforward, because there is a range of interpretations as to what Islam 'says' about the conduct of women and relations between men and women, as well as debates about which attitudes among Muslims are 'properly Islamic', and which attributable to culture. Furthermore, some critics may question the title and structuring of this section as focusing on just one side of the gender divide – on women. Such critics have argued that nearly all notions of what it means to be a woman – that is, of femininity – are constructed in dialogue with some implied or explicit notion of masculinity. Since the two categories are mutually constructed, to look at one without looking at the other is to create an incomplete picture. Also, to group women together with family without explicit consideration of men reinforces the idea that women are inextricably tied to the family and the domestic, whereas men are inherently independent.

Part of the problem is that although publications, television and radio programmes on women and Islam are abundant, very little explicit attention has been paid to 'men and Islam'. In an attempt to redress this balance somewhat, one of the readings we shall examine looks explicitly at sources and interpretations of gender relations in Islamic tradition; another examines how gender relations (among other factors) structure debate about female dress.

Read Ruthven, Chapter 5, 'Introduction', pages 100 to 102, and the boxed text on page 117.

EXERCISE

What are 'patriarchal assumptions' (Ruthven, 2012, 101), and to what extent does Ruthven suggest that Islam is responsible for their presence in Muslim-majority societies?

DISCUSSION

'Patriarchal assumptions' refer to a 'patriarchal family' that is linked to 'extended networks of kin', and in which 'the honour of person and family which is particularly identified with control of women's sexuality, is crucial to the public, social identity of men' (Ruthven, 2012, 101, following Gilsenan, 2000). The extent to which Islam is responsible for this is 'not entirely clear' (Ruthven, 2012, 100). On the one hand the inferiority of women is built into *shari'a* provisions that go back to the Qur'an, including matters such as inheritance and the validity of testimony (although, as we shall see, some argue that these provisions reflect the social and economic conditions of the time, and should not be applied when women can be equal wage-earners and business people). Patriarchal assumptions are also structured into the Arabic language of Islam: for example, '*haram*' (forbidden) is closely related to the area of the household reserved for women (*harim*). However, such assumptions are not exclusive to Muslim-majority societies, and even some of these (in West Africa and South-East Asia) transmit property down the female line. In modernity, the virtuous Islamic woman – contrasted with the 'sexually permissive' Western or Westernised woman – has come to occupy a central role in Islamist rhetoric, mirroring the role of veiled 'repressed' Muslim woman in Western media presentations. □

Read Ruthven, 'Women and the Shari'a', pages 102 to 108, including the boxed texts.

EXERCISE

1 How do traditionalists and modernists agree and differ in their interpretation of the Qur'an's teachings on the treatment of women?

2 What traditional methods have been used to allow flexibility around Qur'anic rules on extra-marital sex, inheritance and polygamous marriage, and how have these impacted on the position of women?

DISCUSSION

1 Both traditionalists and modernists agree that the provisions in the Qur'an against infanticide and the granting to women of some rights of inheritance improved the condition of women compared to the pre-Islamic period (*jahiliya*, or 'ignorance'). But for the traditionalists these provisions – which give women half the inheritance of a man, require two female witnesses to equal one man, and so on – are the final word of God and represent the ideal state, in which women occupy 'equal but different' roles in society. In contrast, modernists argue that the Qur'anic provisions reflect the conditions of the time, and it is the principle behind them that must be honoured rather than the literal word. Hence, whereas half of any brother's provision of inheritance was appropriate for conditions in which there was a clear gender division of labour, in modern urban settings this no longer applies; in this new situation the underlying principle of fairness requires equal inheritance for women.

2 The legal tradition shows considerable flexibility in mediating the impact of Qur'anic prescriptions on social life, with varying consequences for the condition of women. Thus strict laws on illicit sex could be circumvented through the legal fiction (*hila*) of a 'sleeping foetus' – imagining a pregnancy to last up to five, or even seven years – in the case of a deserted or widowed woman. Similarly, a young woman's virginity could be officially preserved even if she got pregnant, through the legal device that she could have been impregnated by semen left by the previous male occupants of public baths. In the case of inheritance, flexibility often worked against women, through legal devices such as the *waqf* (trust) designed to keep property in the patriarchal family. Similarly, the contractual nature of the Islamic marriage can be manipulated by women to their advantage, as in the case of the Prophet's great grand-daughter Sukayna's specifying in her contract that her husband could not practise polygamy. But in practice it has only been women from well-off or powerful families who have been in a position to make use of such opportunities. Two contrasting perspective on the impact of polygamy are presented in Ruthven, pages 105 to 106. ☐

Egyptian and Indonesian attitudes to women, work and child-rearing

Regional and cultural diversity within Muslim-majority societies is demonstrated by the following comparison between Egypt and Indonesia. You have already encountered some comparative data which appeared in Hassan's study *Faithlines* (2002) in Reading 3. (It might be useful to quickly remind yourself of it.) The following tables appear as Tables 6.1 and 6.3 in Hassan (2000).

EXERCISE

What do the tables below tell us about attitudes to women, work and child-rearing in Egypt and Indonesia, and among different groups within them? What does the survey suggest about the difficulties of generalising across Muslim societies, and why should we treat the results of the survey with caution?

Table 6.1 Indonesia: Attitudes towards gender roles by gender, age, education and sample type (%)

	Male	**Female**	**<26 years**	**26–40 years**	**41–55 years**	**>55 years**	**>High school**	**High school, some university**	**Completed university**	**Religious activists**	**Muslim profes-sionals**	**Public**
A working mother can establish as warm and secure a relationship with her children as a mother who does not work	53	70	52	58	59	61	54	56	60	54	63	59
Being a housewife is just as fulfilling as working for pay	79	80	69	80	85	83	80	76	84	77	85	81
Both husband and wife should contribute to household income	69	73	53	70	79	73	77	67	72	65	74	76
On the whole, men make better political leaders than women	62	57	70	59	60	55	50	65	59	68	56	53
If a woman earns more than her husband it is almost certain to cause problems	33	33	46	32	28	29	25	38	29	37	27	30
Higher education is more important for a boy than for a girl	14	8	16	10	11	17	13	15	9	15	10	11

Table 6.3 Egypt: Attitudes towards gender roles by gender, age, education and sample type (%)

	Male	Female	<26 years	26–40 years	41–55 years	>55 years	>High school	High school, some university	Completed university	Religious activists	Muslim profes-sionals	Public
A working mother can establish as warm and secure a relationship with her children as a mother who does not work	28	62	28	31	52	41	40	25	38	16	51	34
Being a housewife is just as fulfilling as working for pay	44	47	39	43	51	51	53	35	46	41	47	47
Both husband and wife should contribute to household income	39	68	42	42	55	55	47	33	47	32	58	40
On the whole, men make better political leaders than women	88	73	76	87	84	84	83	87	85	86	85	81
If a woman earns more than her husband it is almost certain to cause problems	75	61	75	76	67	56	67	68	73	80	64	77
Higher education is more important for a boy than for a girl	57	31	46	53	55	38	50	70	47	59	45	51

Source: Riaz Hassan, Faithlines *(Oxford: Oxford University Press, 2002), 176.*

DISCUSSION

Perhaps the most striking overall finding is that in these similarly pious societies (on the measures of religious observance considered in relation to Reading 3), attitudes towards women, work and child-rearing are quite different. A majority of men and women in Indonesia, including religious activists, believe that a working mother can establish just as good a relationship with her children as a woman who does not work, and agree that both partners should contribute to the household income. They disagree that a woman earning more than a man is 'almost certain to lead to problems', and disagree strongly that higher education is more important for a man than a woman. Only in political leadership are men seen as generally better equipped – and even then by quite a narrow margin.

In Egypt, male attitudes in particular tend to favour women's main role as being in the domestic sphere, and see activities outside the home as damaging this core role. There is also more of a divergence in results between men and women. In these studies, religious activists do not poll very differently from other groups.

The study suggests that caution is needed in generalising about attitudes across Muslim societies, and about singling out religious activists as being very different from other groups. The data we have considered suggest that religion is very significant in the public life of both societies, but this works out differently. The reasons for this are more difficult to discern, and lead us to consider the limitations of the study.

One possible reason ('hypothesis 1') for the Egypt–Indonesia differences is that in Indonesia, Islamic attitudes towards women, work and child-rearing have moved away considerably from traditional patterns; in Egypt this is much less so, although significant minorities favour various forms of gender equality. However, this view rests on the assumption that attitudes in both places began from a common 'traditional' starting point of strict control of women's behaviour, but this may not be so.

Instead ('hypothesis 2') traditions in each location may have been historically quite different, and the surveys are simply a contemporary reflection of this. Ruthven suggests this possibility when, on page 101, he refers to the fact that in South-East Asia 'matrilineal systems of ownership and inheritance predominate', suggesting a rather different attitude towards women's roles from that in Arab societies. On page 113 he goes on to develop this point, writing that 'Among some Muslim communities in South-East Asia, there are no traditions of seclusion'.

So it seems that, on the available evidence, 'hypothesis 2' is more plausible than 'hypothesis 1': the study reflects longstanding cultural differences rather than recent developments. The methodological point here is that contemporary surveys have their limitations: as single snapshots they tell us nothing about developments over time. Also, as we saw earlier, caution is needed in interpreting results because responses to surveys reflect the assumptions and culture of the respondents, which may differ from those of the investigator (and of readers of the study). □

Marriage, divorce and sexuality

Read Ruthven, 'Marriage and divorce', 'Temporary marriage' and 'Islam and sexuality', pages 108 to 112, including the boxed texts.

EXERCISE

1 How do the rights of men and women in marriage and divorce differ?

2 What is temporary marriage (*mut'a*)?

3 What interpretations of Muhammad's multiple marriages have been offered, and how have sexuality and spirituality been linked by Muslim writers?

DISCUSSION

1 In Sunni tradition a woman's guardian is widely recognised as having the right to choose her marriage partner. In Shi'a tradition the woman is regarded as an equal partner, but temporary marriage here may be seen as mitigating that advantage. The husband has greater rights to divorce his wife – this can be done simply by repeated declaration (*talaq*), after waiting a period of three months to determine paternity of any pending offspring. During this time reconciliation may be sought. Women need to provide grounds for divorce, and forfeit their dowry, which may be their only means of support. Custody rights favour men except for young children.

2 This is a device in Shi'ite Islam by which men and women may marry temporarily for sexual purposes. Although critics see it as legalised prostitution, advocates, especially in post-revolutionary Iran, argue that it provides a more structured (and hence protective) context for sexual relations than Western 'free love'.

3 The early Islamic tradition is unapologetic about Muhammad's multiple marriages and sexual prowess – one *hadith* claims he had sex with nine of his wives in a single night. Ruthven links Muhammad's multiple marriages to the figure of the charismatic religious leader, citing Mormonism's polygamous Joseph Smith as another example. However, Christian polemicists have portrayed Muhammad as debauched and sensuous in contrast to the self-controlled, ascetic

Jesus. In response Muslim apologists have emphasised Muhammad's sexual restraint – he remained faithful to just one wife until the age of forty – and have pointed to the practical motivations for polygamy, such as securing tribal alliances and providing for widows in the context of a war in which many men had been killed.

Muslim tradition is strongly affirmative of sexual activity within the context of marriage, although this affirmation tends to be patriarchally structured: men's rights of sexual access to their wives are affirmed in the Qur'an (Ruthven, 2012, 104; surah 2:223 – not 2:222, as incorrectly identified by Ruthven) and *hadiths* (Ruthven, 2012, boxed text on pages 104 and 109–10), but not vice versa. Medieval scholars (such as al-Ghazali) and modern interpreters (such as Bouhdiba) alike regard sexual pleasure as a foretaste of heaven. ☐

Women and gender in a social and political context

EXERCISE

Pause to write down a few words that sum up your own opinion on Islamic attitudes to women's dress. We shall return to this at the end of this section. ☐

Read Ruthven, 'Women in social and religious life', 'Women, colonialism, and the family', 'Sartorial politics' and 'Legal reforms and the backlash against them', on pages 112 to 121.

EXERCISE

1 What is the *mahram* taboo, and what influence has it had on Muslim societies?

2 What influence did colonialism have on gender relations?

3 How do pre-modern Islamic codes of dress differ from the modern 'standardised "Islamic" dress', and how do some Islamists interpret the latter as a sign of women's emancipation? What interpretation does Ruthven offer of this phenomenon?

4 What waves of legal change have followed the colonial period, and how have these affected women?

DISCUSSION

1 The *mahram* taboo forbids married women from mixing with men, except for those male relatives with whom marriage is forbidden. This has drastically limited women's opportunities to move outside the home across much of the Muslim world, and has affected the material culture as well as the social life of Islamic societies: for example, architecturally, as in the construction of housing in Cairo, as shown in Ruthven, Figure 8 on page 114. The influence of this taboo has persisted longer into modernity in the Middle East and South Asia than in Western societies, arguably because of the absence of civil society – organisations and networks between the state and kin – into which women are gradually drawn out of the domestic sphere in Western societies. In most religious ritual there is separation of the sexes, reinforced by taboos on menstruation and childbirth. There are a number of exceptions to this pattern of separation. On page 113, Ruthven argues that in South-East Asia and West Africa there is no tradition of female seclusion – something that we noted in the context of Hassan's (2002) comparison of Egypt and Indonesia. And, as we saw in Abbas' work on popular Sufism in South Asia (Reading 9), men and women mix in some Sufi practices. See also the boxed text on pages 131 to 132 of Ruthven for an example of the difficulties of imposing Arab customs in culturally distant areas.

2 Arguably, colonialism reinforced patriarchal patterns by undermining sources of male prestige external to the family, thus making men more reliant on the family as a source of honour. However, some elite women, influenced by Western ideas, rejected the veil, arguably reinforcing traditional male insecurities.

3 Dress reflected occupation in many pre-modern Islamicate societies, as elsewhere in the world. The 'standardised "Islamic" dress' increasingly worn by Muslim women across the world does not reflect these traditional styles, but rather a post-colonial desire for cultural authenticity, first adopted by the Muslim Sisters (female affiliates of the Muslim Brotherhood) in Egypt in the 1930s. Some Islamists argue that adoption of such dress actually emancipates women into the public sphere, because it enables their participation with men in public settings without them being regarded as sexual objects. Empirical evidence suggests that the reasons for adopting such dress vary.

For the middle classes in many Muslim-majority societies, as for Muslim women in situations where Muslims are a minority, Islamic dress may be chosen as a symbol of religious and cultural identity. But there is also evidence that for some women, adoption of the veil may be a response to male pressure from within the family. In addition, we may note that practical considerations are important – for example, in Bahrain and other Gulf States, middle- and upper-class women may wear the *abbaya* (which conceals the body's shape and covers the head), whereas women working in the fields cannot dress like this for practical reasons. We shall consider the issue of women's dress more fully in the 'Alternative perspectives' section below.

4 There seem to have been two main waves of change – the first liberalising or secularising, which began in the colonial period and may extend well into the subsequent period of post-independence governments. At this time legal reforms tended to bring law codes into line with Western norms: for example, raising the age of permitted marriage. The second wave has involved a return to allegedly (this is, disputed by Islamic modernists and feminists) Islamic norms, such as lowering the age of marriage and reintroducing *hudud* punishments: for example, for adultery. Such measures have been introduced in Iran, Saudi Arabia, the Sudan and Pakistan, although their impact has varied because of differences in the way they have been implemented. *Shari'a* requires either confession or actual witnesses to the event of adultery, standards of proof which in the absence of torture or intimidation of witnesses make conviction very hard to secure. Nevertheless, the widely publicised case of a Nigerian woman who faced death by stoning once her illegitimate baby had been weaned indicates that legal fictions are not always employed. □

Islam and feminism

Read Ruthven, 'Islam and feminism' and 'Conclusion', pages 122 to 125.

EXERCISE

1 What obstacles do Muslim feminists face, and how have they sought to overcome them?

2 What processes are leading Muslim-majority societies to reconsider the role of women in the public domain?

DISCUSSION

1 As we have seen, the almost universal view that the Qur'an is the unchangeable word of God poses a big problem for a small range of issues where gender difference is clearly specified. A modernist hermeneutic, seeking to discern the intention behind the literal word, points to problems with traditional interpretation (such as that

highlighted by Ruthven on page 113, where, as a witness to a business transaction, the testimony of a woman was worth less than that of a man although she had a 'higher degree in business administration'). Attacking patriarchal assumptions that have pervaded the *hadith* tradition is less controversial, and has been pursued by some scholars such as the Moroccan Fatima Mernissi, who points out that many anti-feminist *hadith* stem from Abu Huraira, a Companion of the Prophet whose reliability may be challenged from sources internal to the tradition. Likewise, Egyptian-born Leila Ahmed argues that early Islam was far less patriarchal than 'Abbasid society, when much of the codification of the law occurred, and that this has affected subsequent legal practice. Ahmed argues that this earlier Islam represents an ongoing ethical voice in Islam, at odds with the voice of pragmatic Islam, which largely overlaid it. As we saw in Reading 8, Mernissi takes this duality further back, controversially arguing that the Prophet instituted the *hijab* against his better judgement.

2 Economic change, especially the transition from agrarian to urban, wage-based economies, is putting pressure on women to do waged work, often alongside men, and hence to enter the public domain. Related to this is the increase in mass literacy and mass education, which again is directing women professionally into similar roles to those of men. Ruthven mentions some of the political consequences of these changes in Iran and Saudi Arabia. □

Figure 15 Kuwaiti women posing together, Kuwait City, 1991. Photo: © Peter Turnley/CORBIS.

Alternative perspectives on women and Islam

Rana Kabbani, a Syrian born Muslim, wrote *Letter to Christendom* in response to the lack of understanding of Islam in British society that she felt during the initial controversy surrounding Salman Rushdie's controversial novel *The Satanic Verses*. Her book attempts to provide Western readers with a humane insight into Muslim experience, informed by Kabbani's own experience of being brought up in Syria, and moving to London to study and live. Kabbani does not wear the veil, but here, drawing on the experience of her family, she tries to explain how the politics of the veil developed during the twentieth century, and the different reasons why Muslim women of different generations and in different contexts wear (or do not wear) it.

READING 10

Veiled threats

Perhaps one of the most contentious issues for the West, particularly Western women, is the place of the veil in Islamic culture. In the popular mind in the United States and Europe, the veil covering the face is the symbol of Islam. Yet it is worth recalling that it is of Christian origin, and was adopted by the Arabs only when they conquered Syria in the seventh century in imitation of the social elite they found there and displaced. The veil should not be confused with the Islamic *hijab* which covers a woman's hair, considered sexually attractive and arousing. During the Prophet's lifetime even the *hijab* was worn only by his wives in order to distinguish them from other women. It was later taken on by Muslim women in emulation of these 'Mothers of Islam'. The Qur'an enjoins modesty of apparel, so as not to reveal to men outside her family a woman's hair, her naked limbs or her bosom.

Earlier this century, some relaxation of the rules of modesty crept into Muslim practice here and there, particularly in countries with secular governments. But where change occurred, it met with resistance. When the miniskirt came in and I was allowed to wear one, my paternal grandmother, who never appeared in public without a *hijab*, was aghast. 'The knee is shameful,' she would mutter. And when, aged ten, on the way to the swimming pool, I once ran into the kitchen at home wearing a bathing costume, our aged cook nearly dropped her pot, exclaiming to my mother, 'Aren't you ashamed to let your daughter appear naked in front of men!' When she got no satisfactory reply, she complained to my father. He calmed her down by reminding her that the Prophet himself had urged Muslims to teach their children, girls and boys alike, to swim, hunt and ride horses.

My paternal grandmother's 'at home' days were occasions when I could observe the rituals of traditional female behaviour. These occasions were the pattern in poor as well as bourgeois homes, where women met together and enjoyed each other's company away from the pressures of their households. The mornings were spent in preparation in my grandmother's house: vats of lemonade were made with grated peel; bowls of custard were laid out to cool in the dark pantry; and everything was cleaned a dozen times: the floors swept and then scrubbed with soap and water, the chests dusted then rubbed with oil to make the marquetry stand out, and the divan covers freshly laundered and starched. Sugared almonds were piled in dishes and *nargilehs* set out for those elderly ladies who smoked and whose disapproving husbands were dead.

The women entered the house by the harem door and, once safely inside the rooms reserved for them, took off their *hijab* and street coats. For the rest of the afternoon that part of the house was strictly out of bounds to men, allowing the guests to relax. Many were wearing their finery, their hair shaped with curling tongs and their eyes ringed with *kohl*. Bare arms and *décolleté* dresses were displayed. Some had brought their unwed daughters, since others had come to find brides for their unmarried sons. The newly betrothed (whether rich or poor) would wear their in-laws' gifts of jewellery for all to admire. Some carried lutes or tambourines to entertain the company while others would sing, dance, or tell stories. The more devout would deliver a religious homily.

My maternal grandmother was a very different story. Her upper-class family wore their religion lightly. Two generations ago, between the two world wars, educated Muslim women like her were flamboyantly tearing off the *hijab*. For maximum publicity, such luminaries of the feminist movement in Egypt as Huda Sha'rawi and Durriya Shafiq dropped their headscarves over the rail of ships or threw them out of the windows of trains as they returned to the Muslim world from Europe. Compared to the secular and scientific West, their own societies seemed stagnant, suffocating and tradition-bound. They had been impressed by the suffragette movement and modelled their own liberation on it.

In the wider political arena, these early Arab feminists agreed with their men that to throw off colonial rule, Western methods had to be adopted because they seemed to hold the key to strength. The most ardent nationalists, those who had suffered most from Western domination, still felt drawn to Western culture.

Across the Arab world, the daughters of this revolutionary generation managed to lead lives not unlike those of Western women of the more affluent classes: going to university, finding jobs in the professions, marrying for love, and bringing up their own families in the modern way. Western fashions were assiduously followed: the New Look was as much 'in' in Damascus as it was in Paris. In the courtyards of the old houses, upper-class men and women danced to the latest tangos and foxtrots on the gramophone; while Western art was admired and studied, influencing style as much as it did in Europe.

When my parents got married in 1956, 'Cubist' furniture was all the rage, so to accommodate their voguish bedroom suite – side tables shaped like Braque guitars and Picasso motifs on the curtains – they threw out (to their later regret) the traditional furnishings of damasked brocade and the bridal chests inlaid with mother-of-pearl.

These trends grew out of a new post-war prosperity, out of the emergence of an educated middle class, out of a widely shared hope that the revolutionary upheavals then shaking the region would lead to political renewal with greater popular participation. Nasser was the hero of the hour. Whenever he spoke, people across the Arab world would be glued to their radios, and when he nationalised the Suez Canal in 1956, crowds ran shouting with excitement into the streets in a spontaneous celebration of the new era.

There was a sense that the whole 'Third World' was awakening and that it had a future which it would fashion itself. Nasser was one of a pantheon which included Nehru, Nkruma, Sukarno – proud leaders who for the first time represented the interests and aspirations of their people. This was the heyday of nationalism. Algeria's eight-year war of independence against France, a classic armed struggle against colonial rule, aroused enormous passions.

One of the heroines of this struggle was Jamila Bouhired, who had been tortured and scarred by her French captors but had inspired a whole generation of Algerian women to become freedom fighters in the war of a 'million martyrs'. In the early sixties, when the war was over, she paid an official visit to Kuwait, where the Minister of Education and a party of veiled women teachers waited to receive her at the airport. She appeared at the door of the plane – with her hair uncovered. Not wishing to embarrass her, and no doubt infected by the spirit of the times, the Minister turned to the teachers and commanded: 'Quick, take off your *hijab*!'

Much has changed today. It would be inconceivable for an official in a Muslim country to order women to remove their *hijab* without starting a riot. This is not only because of the rise of fundamentalism; it is primarily because the *hijab* is no longer seen as a symbol of an archaic tradition. Rather, it has become a striking affirmation of identity – religious, cultural and political – reflecting the more radical feelings that now prevail.

The adoption of the *hijab* by educated and politicised young women, often from secular families, has in the 1980s become an inescapable phenomenon of life in most Muslim cities. There are many reasons for this, but above all it reflects the disillusion of this generation with the achievements of its elders. In the Arab world, independence proved an immense disappointment. No new social order founded on justice was created: instead, corruption and repression ruled. Defeat in war led to the loss of yet more lives and land. Despite Arab rhetoric Israeli hegemony, propped up by the West, remained unchallenged. 'Third World' solidarity collapsed. In Arabia and the Gulf, the very areas where oil wealth in independent Arab hands could have made a difference, Western interests rather than Arab aspirations seemed to prevail. Western products of all sorts, cultural as well as material, flooded the marketplace.

Responding to these setbacks, Muslim feminists no longer choose to model themselves on their Western sisters. The over-permissive West – which they now perceive, perhaps crudely, as exploitative of women, as plagued by drugs and AIDS, and as indifferent to the sufferings of the rest of the world – is to them a less attractive place than it seemed to their grandmothers. At the risk of reiterating what has now become a cliché, it must also be said that the issues which concern them are not those of Western feminists. In the late 1970s a conference was held in Scandinavia on International Women's Day. Among the Arabs present was the Palestinian guerrilla fighter Fatima Barnawi, who had spent long years in Israeli jails, was tortured, and had been forced to watch her father being tortured when no information could be extracted from her. I recall her bewilderment when, newly arrived at the conference, she was exposed to hour-long speeches by European feminists on lesbian rights. Although the importance of debates about sexuality in the context of Western feminism should not be underestimated, the political exigencies of survival in the Middle East could not help but make these issues seem a luxury.

When Arabs today view their society – and much the same could be said for all Muslims – they see a travesty of modernism, neither genuinely Western nor properly Eastern, and certainly not satisfactory. The frenzy of Islamic revivalism must surely be a reaction to this state of affairs. The women who decide to put on the *hijab*, that flag of Islamic commitment, are not retreating from ground won by their grandmothers. Just as it was a political choice fifty years ago to remove the *hijab*, a choice freely made and of great consequence, so the decision today to put it on again is equally momentous and equally political.

These women are not withdrawing to an archaic past, nor do they wish to stay demurely at home. Most often they are professional women, doctors, teachers, pharmacists and lawyers. Politically, they are activists – a sort of Muslim Sisterhood not unlike the Muslim Brotherhood of male militants, but unconnected with it. The wearing of Islamic dress gives these women greater rather than less freedom and mobility, for in such austere garb and with the mentality that accompanies it, they are much less likely to be closely monitored by their families.

Wearing the *hijab* can be a liberation, freeing women from being sexual objects, releasing them from the trap of Western dress and the dictates of Western fashion. Just as feminists in the West have reflected on the connection between 'feminine' clothes and female oppression, so Muslim feminists reject the outward symbols of sexual allure. In favour of the *hijab* it can be said that by distancing its wearer from the world, it enriches spiritual life, grants freedom from material preoccupations, and erases class differences by expressing solidarity with others in the same uniform. Since all women look the same in it, it is a most effective equaliser, and since it camouflages rich clothing, it is in keeping with the Islamic injunction against ostentation. The long dull coat usually worn with the *hijab* is of similar significance and may be compared with the dun-coloured cloak favoured in Renaissance Florence after the passing of the anti-luxury laws.

I have had occasion to observe the *hijab* phenomenon closely because my own cousin, Lama, took to it at the age of sixteen. Her grandmother, the wife of the prime minister of Syria in the 1950s, had thrown it off in her youth. Lama's mother studied law at university, practised at the Bar, and was the first woman in Syria to run a television talk show. She was an attractive young woman with a successful career, who had married the man she loved and was independent, liberated and Westernised in the tradition of the women in her family. Lama's decision was therefore met with considerable shock and disapproval – all the more so when it became apparent that for my cousin, the wearing of the *hijab* meant a commitment to a certain form of Islamic activism. Gradually the family adapted to what she had become, but it was always intriguing to visit them and find one daughter dressed like an Islamic nun, her head tied in a scarf, wearing opaque stockings and long-sleeved garment even in midsummer, with nothing showing but her face and hands, while her two sisters were barebacked in sundresses.

Some practical advantage may be derived from the *hijab*. Western feminists are familiar with the notion of a supportive group of friends, acquaintances and contacts – a female alternative to the exclusive 'old boy' network – and so it is with their Muslim sisters. In most Muslim countries – in Morocco, Algeria, Libya, Tunisia, Egypt, Sudan and Nigeria; in Jordan; in the occupied West Bank and Gaza; in Lebanon and Syria; in the Gulf; in Turkey, Iran, Afghanistan and Pakistan; in

Malaysia and Indonesia – something like a women's underground is taking shape, providing an alternative to the apparatus of power and influence which in all these countries belongs to the state and to those most closely associated with it.

Source: Rana Kabbani, Letter to Christendom *(London: Virago, 1992), 22–8.*

EXERCISE

1 Where did the Islamic practice of veiling originate? What distinction does Kabbani make between the veil and the *hijab*?

2 What influence did class make to attitudes to women's dress in Syria in the 1950s?

3 What phases have women's wearing of the *hijab* gone through since, and why have these changes come about?

DISCUSSION

1 It is claimed that the practice of veiling was adopted by Arab Muslims from Syrian Christians (although, in fact, it was found also in ancient Egyptian, Hellenic and Jewish culture; see El Guindi, 1999). In Kabbani's terminology 'the veil' covers the face, the *hijab* only covers the hair. We shall see that the terminology of 'veiling' is quite complex and confusing.

2 Middle-class and poor families in post-war Syria seem to have practised separation of men and women – Kabbani points to the positive side of the social life this afforded women in her paternal grandmother's family. In contrast, the women in her upper-class maternal grandmother's family had stopped wearing the *hijab* in the interwar period as a sign of modernity and emancipation, and by the 1950s Kabbani's mother and her well-off and educated friends enjoyed a lifestyle similar to their Western counterparts. Among their classes, wearing the *hijab* came to be seen as unacceptable – illustrated in the Kuwaiti minister's response to the visiting Algerian minister.

3 Since the 1960s this situation has changed, such that the next generation of educated young women, who in the 1950s would not wear the *hijab*, were by the 1980s adopting it. Kabbani suggests a variety of reasons for this. These include disillusionment with progress in Arab countries since independence, and a perception of Western models that were being followed as favouring Western interests and over-permissiveness, as with the break described between Muslim and Western feminists. Practically, adopting the *hijab*

can bring some social benefits, perhaps reducing unwanted male attention and giving access to networks of women's solidarity and influence. □

The following extracts come from a recent study by Sofie Anne Roald, a Norwegian convert to Islam. Her book, *Women in Islam: The Western Experience*, concentrates on women of Arab origin living in Western Europe. It looks especially at the influence of Islamism from the Arab world on the interpretations of this group, and at their development of the Islamist tradition, which she argues is increasingly influential across the Muslim world. The book looks at the primary sources (Qur'an and *hadith*), classical commentaries, and modern interpretations. It considers issues including perceptions of women, gender relations, women's political participation, polygamy (marrying more than one person at once), divorce and child custody, female circumcision and dress. The extracts here focus on gender relations and female dress, though they also raise the issue of why it is that male dress, though important in the *hadith* literature, is almost entirely absent from contemporary debates.

READING 11

Gender relations

In the Koran, little is said about gender relations. The most explicit injunctions are given in verse 4:34, the same verse which states the social role of men as breadwinners of the family. The verse in Ali's translation says: 'Men are the protectors and maintainers of (*quwwamun 'ala*) women, because God has given the one more (strength) than the other, and because they support them from their means'.[16]

In Asad's translation it says:

> Men shall take full care of women with the bounties which God has bestowed more abundantly on the former than on the latter, and with what they may spend out of their possessions.[17]

The American Islamic feminist and Muslim scholar, Amina Wadud-Muhsin, who is a convert to Islam, has investigated various historical and contemporary Islamic scholars' interpretations of this verse. She indicates that the understanding of *qiwama* as men's control over

[16] Ali, A. (1989) *The Holy Qur'an: Text, Translation, and Commentary*, Brentwood, Middlesex, Amana, 195.

[17] Asad, M. (1984) *The Message of the Qur'an*, translated and explained by Muhammad Asad, Gibraltar, al-Andalus, 109.

women is subject to time and place. She proposes a contemporary interpretation of the verse whereby men's responsibility for women applies only to their economic support of the family. With changes in the socio-economic system, she sees room for a more 'liberal' reinterpretation (Wadud-Muhsin 1992 [trans. 1999]).[18]

The same verse also contains the most controversial statement regarding men's relationship to women. The verse continues:

> And for those women whose disloyalty and ill-conduct (*nushuz*) you have reason to fear, admonish them [first]; then leave them alone in bed [second]; then hit them [third]. And if thereupon they pay you heed (*ata'nakum*), do not seek to harm them. Behold, God is indeed most high, great.

I have observed that the first part of the verse is frequently referred to by common Muslims as well as by Islamists, whereas they tend not to mention the last part. On the other hand, some non-Muslims, particularly within 'popular Orientalism' in western countries, tend to refer to the verse as a whole in order to portray Islam as a religion hostile towards women.

In contrast to this verse, Islamists refer to other passages in the Koran which indicate a more intimate and close relationship between men and women:

1. 'The believing men and the believing women are protectors (*awliya'*) to each other' (K. 9:71).
2. 'It is He who has created you out of one living entity, and out of it brought into being its mate, so that man might incline [with love] towards woman' (K. 7:189).
3. 'And among His signs is this: He created for you mates from among yourselves so that you might incline towards them and he endangers love (*mawadda*) and mercy (*rahma*)' (K. 30:21).
4. 'The rights of the wives [with regard to their husbands] are equal to the [husbands' rights] over them [with regard to divorce]' (K. 2:228).
5. 'And consort with your wives in kindness (*ma'ruf*), for if you dislike them, it may well be that you dislike something which God has made a source of abundant good' (K. 4:19).
6. 'Your women are a tilth for you, so go to your tilth as you will, and send [good deeds] before you for your souls, and have

[18] Wadud-Muhsin, A. (1999) *Qur'an and Woman: Re-reading the Sacred Text from a Woman's Perspective*, Oxford, Oxford University Press (first published 1992).

> God-consciousness. For know that you will meet Him. Give glad tidings to the believers' (K. 2:223).

In the hadith-literature there is a similar picture. In some places, the relationship between men and women is portrayed as one of love and intimacy, whereas in other places, women are described in terms which for westerners born and raised in times with a strong notion of gender equality might appear as degrading and disparaging of women as a whole.

Source: Anne Sofie Roald, Women in Islam: The Western Experience *(London and New York: Routledge, 2001), 145–6.*

EXERCISE

How have commentators differed in their interpretation of Qur'an 4:34? According to Roald, what is the relationship between men and women in the Qur'an and *hadith* literature?

DISCUSSION

Perhaps surprisingly, the Qur'an says little about gender relations, and most discussion has surrounded the single verse 4:34. The first part of the verse gives men a duty of care (*qiwama*) for women, for reasons of greater male endowment or strength. Feminist interpreters (such as Amina Wadud-Muhsin) interpret this protective role and its basis in what God has given in the context of economic conditions, and therefore as subject to change with changing economic patterns. In contrast, most interpreters have seen these differences as natural and therefore not subject to change. The second half of the verse appears to authorise men to punish women, including hitting them. Not surprisingly, Islamists and other Muslims tend to focus on the first part of the verse, critics of Islam on the second part. To balance the negative impression the second part of the verse may create, Muslims are likely to refer to a range of other verses in the Qur'an which set 4:34 in context. Thus, 9:71 stresses mutuality ('protectors to each other'), 2:228 equal rights to divorce, and 7:189 and 30:21 their common origin and qualities of love and mercy. According to Roald, the same kind of balance between material that stresses mutuality and tenderness and 'degrading' representations of women from an egalitarian perspective are found in the *hadith* literature. □

Mixing with non-family members

READING 11 CONTINUED

There are four passages in particular in the Koran which are regarded as dealing with behaviour between men and women who mix outside kinship bonds:

1 Tell the believing men to lower their gaze and to be mindful of the chastity [guard their private parts]. This will be most conducive to their purity. Verily, God is aware of what you do.

And tell the believing women to lower their gaze and to be mindful of their chastity [guard their private parts], and to not display their adornment beyond what may [decently] be apparent thereof. Let then draw their coverings [*khumur*; sing. *khimar*] over their bosoms and let them not display their adornments to any but their husbands, or their fathers ... Let them not stamp their feet so as to reveal what they hide of their adornments. O believers, turn unto God all of you so that you may succeed (K. 24:30–1).

2 Women, advanced in years, who do not hope for marriage, incur no sin if they discard their garments (*thiyabahunna*), provided they do not aim at a showy display of their charm. But it is better for them to abstain from this. God is All-hearing All-knowing (K. 24:60).

3 O Prophet! Tell your wives and your daughters and the wives of the believers, that they should draw over themselves some of their outer garment (*jilbab*). That will be better, so that they will be recognised and not annoyed. God is ever Forgiving Merciful (K. 33:59).

4 O you who believe! Enter not the Prophet's dwellings unless you are given leave ... and [as for the Prophet's wives] when you ask of them anything that you need, ask them from behind a curtain (*hijab*). That is purer for your hearts and for their hearts. You should not cause annoyance to the Messenger of God and you should not ever marry his wives after him. That would, in the sight of God, be an enormity (K. 33:53).

The first three Koranic passages above are directed towards women in general. The fourth passage deals with how men should behave towards the wives of the Prophet only.

Source: Anne Sofie Roald, Women in Islam: The Western Experience, *255.*

QUESTION

What restrictions do these Qur'anic passages place on men and women mixing with non-family members?

DISCUSSION

Both genders should cover their genitals, and women should conceal their breasts and decorations such as jewellery (24:30–1). Fewer restrictions are placed on older women (24:60). Muslim women should wear some kind of outer garment to enable them to be recognised as Muslims and avoid harassment (33:59). In 33:53 a special case seems to be made for the wives of Muhammad, who should be separated behind a curtain (*hijab* – the origin of this term in Islamic discourse). □

The last two passages concern classical and contemporary debates on Islamic dress, and mention a number of commentators from both periods. You do not need to know anything in detail about these people, but they give you an idea of the kind of arguments that current Muslims, especially Islamists, engage in.

READING 11 CONTINUED

The Islamic debate on veiling

The four law schools differ concerning female veiling. Three of the law schools, Shafi'i, Maliki and Hanbali promote the view that the face-veil is obligatory [...]. In the Hanafi law school, however, the face-veil is not obligatory.

[...]

Contemporary Islamic literature

With regard to classical commentators on the Koran, there is a consensus that women should cover in one way or another. The controversy between the scholars is the extent to which women should cover: should a woman cover her hair but expose the face and the hands, should she cover everything except for one eye, or should the covering be complete? Contemporary scholars are involved in the same controversy. Among Islamic scholars there is consensus with regard to female covering but there is no consensus for the actual form of covering. [...]

ash-Sha'rawi points out that every Muslim woman *should* wear a head-cover, whereas he regards a face-veil as necessary only for a women whose face is so beautiful that she might cause temptation (*fitna*). This view is common among Muslims in general. The problem which arises is who should define this beauty and what degree of beauty actually causes temptation. I believe this idea has arisen in parallel with the idea of women as temptresses. As I have not often encountered the idea of women as temptresses in Arab Islamism, I find it interesting that in ash-Sha'rawi's book this idea is prominent. He states that 'the whole issue [of head-cover and face-veil] circles around the fact that women should not be *fitna* to men' (ash-Sha'rawi, n.d.: 97 [translation mine]). ash-Sha'rawi does not represent the Islamist movements but rather he is *madhhabist* (i.e. he adheres to one Islamic law school), and he thus represents a traditional understanding of Islam. It is interesting to note that in verse 33:59 the Koran mentions that women should cover so as not to be molested *by* men, whereas ash-Sha'rawi has turned the whole issue around to suggest that women should cover so as not to be temptations *to* men. I believe that the way these ideas are presented is decisive in the formation of attitudes. In the former case men are the aggressors and women the victims, whereas in the latter, women are the actors and men the victims. However, as I have discussed before we should bear in mind the possible change in cultural content of a concept in the translation process, and it might be the 'western cultural base pattern' which makes me interpret ash-Sha'rawi's argument in such a way.

Source: Anne Sofie Roald, Women in Islam: The Western Experience, *267, 271–2.*

EXERCISE

1 How have the four law schools differed in their views on veiling?

2 How have contemporary Islamic commentators interpreted the Qur'anic teaching on women's covering?

DISCUSSION

1 The four main Sunni law schools offer different guidance on the face veil, with three considering it obligatory, and the more liberal and most widespread Hanafi school considering it not obligatory.

2 As with classical scholarship, there is a consensus that women should cover up, but not on the actual form covering should take. For example, ash-Sha'rawi argues that every woman should cover her head, but only a woman so attractive as to be a source of temptation to men (the word *fitna* here means 'source of strife') needs to wear a face covering. Roald argues that this common understanding reverses the Qur'anic identification of the source of trouble, making a woman's beauty responsible, whereas the Qur'an places responsibility on men as potential molesters. However, Roald admits that her

reading may be due to her 'western cultural base pattern', or preconceptions with which she approaches the readings. ☐

Male dress in Islam

The topic of women's dress in Islam is much discussed, but what of male dress? Roald comments:

> It is amazing how Islamic writers tend to concentrate on female dress. Given that male dress is a major theme in the hadith literature, one might expect that there would be much written about it in the contemporary Islamic movement, particularly as there is an obvious conflict between the guidelines given in the hadiths and how male Muslims dress today. However, I have rarely found anything written about how men should dress in general. Writings on male dress tend to be paragraphs dealing with the prohibition against men wearing silk and the special dress men should wear during Hajj, incorporated in general books on Islam. In contrast, books on 'proper female Islamic dress' have flooded the market.
>
> (Roald, 2001, 267)

The almost exclusive focus on women's dress may be because, as Ruthven suggests on pages 115 to 116, with the collapse of Muslim power in the public sphere in the colonial period, the domestic sphere became the focus of Islamic identity. However, the Qur'an and the *hadith* both have a lot to say about male dress, and an internet search on the topic 'Islamic dress' will reveal numerous sites devoted to appropriate dress for Muslim men, as well as those concerning proper female attire.

Men, like women, are expected to be modest in dress; they should always be loosely covered from the navel to the knee in public, and they should not wear tight, sheer, revealing or eye-catching clothing. The Pakistani *salwar kameez*, consisting of baggy trousers with a long, loose, long-sleeved top is traditional, appropriate male attire, or a long, loose-fitting gown has often been preferred in parts of the Middle East and North Africa. As numerous *hadith* refer to the Prophet wearing the turban, many consider this an important symbol of identity, as well as demonstrating modesty, and there are different styles of wearing the turban. There are *hadith* forbidding the wearing of women's clothes by men (and vice versa) and the imitation of unbelievers and other religious groups' styles of clothing – for example, the belt around a loose flowing garment worn by Christian monks. There is thus some debate about whether the wearing of jeans should be forbidden to Muslims, since these could be seen as typical of unbelievers and Christians, and they can also be tight-fitting and revealing.

If male dress generally tends to be less commented upon than female dress, anthropologist Fadwa El Guindi makes the point that 'A crucial, neglected and overlooked fact about veiling is the clear evidence that men in Arab society veil', and that 'the Prophet Muhammad himself face-veiled on certain occasions' (El Guindi, 1999, 117). Thus El Guindi would argue that pictures showing the Prophet with a veiled face are not simply employing an artistic device to avoid showing his facial features, but are accurate reflections of this male veiling tradition. Veiling, she claims, is a sophisticated device traditionally connected with modesty and status in both men and women.

El Guindi gives one example of modest male, dress-related behaviour that occurred on the campus of the 'secular' 'Ain Shams University in Cairo, when a male visitor, coming to the women's lounge to discuss the Qur'an, knocked on the door :

> The women scrambled for their *hijabs* and *qina's*. ... I looked out of the door and saw a man in a *gallabiyyah* (an ankle-length white, unfitted gown with long sleeves). He pulled his *kufiyya* (head shawl) over his face and entered very cautiously, literally rubbing against the wall trying not to look in the direction of the women until he reached a curtain diagonally hung in the corner of the room. He went behind it and sat facing the women from behind the curtain. That is, it was the man who both face-veiled and sat behind the *hijab* (curtain).
>
> (El Guindi, 1999, 118)

El Guindi's fascinating study challenges some common assumptions for, as she points out, to regard veiling as 'a unique or isolated woman's phenomenon' (1999, 117) is potentially misleading: 'We cannot comprehend a phenomenon by leaving out an entire sex' (1999, 118).

Islamic dress: conclusion

It should be obvious by now that 'Islamic dress' is not one, monolithic phenomenon. There are historical and cultural variations, and very different views of appropriate dress. For example, during fieldwork in Malaysia, Bowman found very clearly articulated distinctions between Islamic behaviour and Arab custom. Many Malaysians had observed Saudi society through making the *hajj*, and felt discomfort with the lifestyle and dress codes enforced upon women there. It was 'Arab' rather than 'Islamic' for women to be completely covered, some thought, pointing out that Saudi women actually have to remove some of their coverings to be appropriately dressed for the *hajj*. One Malaysian woman commented, 'It is not what you wear, it is how you behave that makes you a Muslim' (Bowman, 1994). At the other extreme, ethnologist

Annelies Moors (2003) points out that for Yemeni women, adopting the *abaya* (the loose black garment that covers head and body, common in the Gulf) is a new fashion that involves *less* covering than traditional Yemeni female garb.

It is important to remember that there are dress codes for both men and women, and that there is a considerable, lucrative and growing Islamic female and male fashion industry, offering a variety of regional styles from Morocco to Indonesia, and a growing range of hybrid fashions (see Moors, 2003). However, before leaving the subject of dress, we should note the *hadith* that states: 'he who wears clothes of pride in this world will be dressed in humiliating clothes in the next life.'

EXERCISE

Go back to your initial opinions on Islamic women's dress. Have any of your views changed? What additional points or arguments would you make now if you were asked to describe the issues? □

10
The two *jihads*

Read Ruthven, Chapter 6, 'Introduction' to 'The two *Jihads*', on pages 126 to 128.

EXERCISE

How did the classical doctrine of *jihad* develop, and what historical conditions informed its development?

DISCUSSION

The word *jihad* means 'struggle', which originally included all kinds of efforts to further the cause of Islam, rather than just military efforts. Unlike the individual obligations of the Five Pillars, *jihad* is a collective obligation, and can be undertaken by the ruler on behalf of the whole community. The classical doctrine developed during the main initial phase of the Islamic conquest, and its form reflects those conditions in the rapid expansion of the Islamic empire up to 750 CE). Thus the expansion of the 'rule of Islam' (*dar al-Islam*) until it encompasses the entire world is envisaged, and the world beyond categorised as the 'place of war' (*dar al-harb*) until Islamic rule is extended there too. Initially, only temporary truces (*dar al-sulh*) with enemies were accepted, but gradually, as Islamic expansion faltered, this condition became recognised as semi-permanent. This category has recently been revived by Muslims trying to re-think the relationship between the Muslim-majority world and the West. Under Islamic rule, 'People of the Book' (Jews and Christians), and later Zoroastrians and Hindus, were recognised minorities with limited rights permitted on payment of a poll tax. □

Post September 11th reflections

'Jihadist' groups and resources of reconciliation in Islam

The idea of *jihad* as 'holy war', and especially of the *shahid*, the warrior slain in battle ensuring his (or sometimes her) place in paradise, has attained great prominence in the last few years (to 2004), partly as a result of suicide bombings in Israel and Chechnya, but especially because of the attacks on Washington and New York on September 11th, 2001. The term '*jihadist*' has come to be used of those Muslim groups dedicated to violent struggle. The reading below comes from a book authored by the brother of the so-called 'Twentieth September 11th bomber' – Zacarias Moussaoui – who was detained prior to the attack because police in Florida became suspicious of his activities. He remains (in 2012) detained in a US jail. In this reading, Samad Moussaoui explains some of the factors that led to his brother's involvement in *jihadist* activities, and in particular the recruiting techniques of Saudi-funded Wahhabist groups. Following the Kharijite and Wahhabi traditions, these groups take the view that to be a Muslim it is not enough simply to say the *shahada*; rather a high degree of religious observance and dedication is required, and those who do not meet their standards are regarded as not properly Muslim at all – indeed, as potential targets for violent *jihad*.

READING 12

Looking for an identity

At home, Aïcha [mother] never spoke to us in Arabic. So we felt out of place even among North Africans, not knowing their language. When we asked our mother to teach us a few words, she would laugh at our accent and our lousy pronunciation – so we stopped asking. Our sisters, of course, were born in Morocco and went back there almost every year – they spoke Arabic. But when Zac and I met Moroccan families, they would feel sorry for us. 'Oh, they don't speak Arabic? *Meskeen!* Poor things!' And my mother would respond, 'No they don't, they're right little French boys, those two.'

Neither did our mother teach us about Arab ways and customs, or about Muslim culture. Not because she wasn't acquainted with that culture, but because she didn't want to teach us. She was quoted recently as saying, 'I made sure they didn't hang out with Arabs.'[19] Zac and I asked her several times how you prayed and why. She dodged the question. She told us it wasn't what people of our age did. Yet, since Mulhouse [...], we'd seen our friends going to the mosque with their fathers. So why not us? We felt ridiculous in the company of others. Who might have told us all about these things? Not our father, who wasn't a practising Muslim, even if he had been around. Not our aunts and uncles, who all lived on the other side of the Mediterranean. So we decided to ask Saïd, our mother's partner, who was a practising Muslim.

We saw him bowing, getting up, and kneeling back down again. We wanted to know what it all meant, what was the meaning of the words he uttered. In a kind, if slightly awkward, way he gave us the relevant books, not knowing how to explain it all himself. We didn't understand the first thing about it. The books explained in concrete terms how to

[19] *Le Monde*, 27 September 2001.

pray, but didn't give us any spiritual information. There wasn't a mosque in Narbonne. There was a prayer hall at St. Jean-St. Pierre, but I didn't know that until much later. Like lots of prayer halls, there was no sign on the street. It was discreet, in an ordinary apartment.

There was no way that we could ask our North African friends anything, because that would expose our terrible lack of culture, and they would have really teased us. Zac and I met discouragement at every turn, until we gave up our quest. I was twenty-one when I went into a mosque for the first time, in Montpellier. I think the first mosque Zacarias entered was in Great Britain. I believe that this religious ignorance has had a huge impact on his life, and that the same is true for people drawn to the al-Qaeda training camps in Pakistan, and for French prisoners at Guantanamo Bay.

At this juncture, I'd like to interrupt my story and say one or two things which seem crucial to any understanding of Zacarias' subsequent actions.

There are now more than one billion people in the world who adhere to Islam. Ninety-five percent of them are Sunnis. Four percent are Shi'ites. Slightly more than a million are Wahhabi, but this particular million is disproportionately wealthy, because Wahhabism is the state religious ideology of Saudi Arabia, which possesses the world's largest confirmed oil reserves.[20]

Part of the appeal of Wahhabism is that it offers a reply to international horrors. The state of the world is disturbing, with the war in Chechnya and its appalling massacres, or the fallout of the war waged by the Russians in Afghanistan. (Zacarias and I felt tremendous admiration for the late Shah Ahmad Massoud, a hero of the war with Russia who would later lead the 'Northern Alliance' against the Taliban.) Bosnia underwent ethnic cleansing, which Zac and I saw as a systematic extermination, genocide taking place before our very eyes. And then there is Algeria, something of a special case in the litany of bloodshed: more than 100,000 dead in ten years. A civilian population massacred. Last, Palestine is under occupation. The Palestinians live under a system of apartheid.

For any young North African living in France, all this horror is intolerable and exacerbates feelings that are already greatly bruised by overtly expressed discrimination against Arabs and Muslims. We are actually easy prey to bigots because our vulnerability is well-known. No voices are being raised to give vent to or to defend our feelings. One-track thinking rules, and nobody dares speak out.

[20] These numbers on the branches of Islam are the subject of debate. In particular, some estimates of the number of Wahhabi adherents are five or even ten times greater.

In Montpellier, Zacarias made friends with students who came from a tough neighbourhood called Petit-Bard, and from the Paillade projects. These students explained to him that what was going on in Algeria was a legitimate struggle against corrupt leaders and injustices, and that the fighters in this struggle were called the *mujaheddin*. Their analysis seemed very odd to us: Algeria being a land of Islam, how could you make war in the name of Islam against other Muslims? Women, children, young men and old, beheaded with axes, throats slit with saws! That couldn't have been done in the name of Islam. All these atrocities were to be condemned in no uncertain terms.

Nowadays in France, when a young Muslim becomes interested in learning about his religion, wants to find out about his parents' values and the history of the community, and his parents can't provide answers, he is likely to turn to a cultural or religious association. He goes to Arab-Muslim bookshops, as well as traditional bookshops. In the latter, the material is often quite expensive, and geared to an intellectual readership. Furthermore, the books are often written by Orientalists. The Arab-Muslim bookshops tend to be friendlier and more easy-going, and less expensive. You can find plenty of things evoking your parents' culture: the same perfume; the same clothes; *soubhahs* and *siwaks;*[21] magazines; tapes and videos for learning Arabic; the Koran; and books about the foundations of Islam, religious practices, the history of the Arab World, and Arab Muslim culture. Books of every shape and size.

The young Muslim may also be approached by *tablighs*[22] whom you can meet by chance in markets. He might attend the fair organized by the French Union of Islamic Organizations [UOIF]. There he will find all kinds of products: clothes, perfumes – anything and everything that can be traded. Or he might sign up for a religious course conducted by the Association of Islamic Welfare Projects in France [APBIF], which also organizes religious festivals such as the commemoration of the birth of the Prophet Muhammad [Peace be Upon Him]. The landscape for a young novice is like rich, uncultivated terrain. His first steps are haphazard. During religious meetings, people may bring up trivial or secondary subjects year after year, making others think that they are the crucial questions. Quite by chance the novice may stumble upon an extremely vitriolic book, or an especially understated book. He may find authentic religious instruction – or political and sectarian indoctrination.

[21] Soubhahs: prayer beads. A siwak is a wooden twig that is used to clean your teeth. It might be from an olive or palm tree, but the best siwaks come from the arak tree.

[22] Members of a pietistic movement founded in 1927; by nature it is missionary, proselytizing and radically anti-fundamentalist.

In the absence of any informed parental authority or clearly defined religious authority, the young novice is left to his own devices. And danger lurks everywhere. A lot of those talking in the name of religion are in no way qualified to do so. The main criteria for imams are quite simply knowledge of Arabic, and an ability to step up into the *minbar*, or pulpit, to speak. (Sometimes imams are required to know the Koran by heart, but no-one ever asks any questions about the real nature of their theological studies.) The first generation of immigrants had two concerns: finding places of worship, and having someone available to teach Arabic and the Koran to their children. But when those entrusted with these responsibilities are novices, there is no telling what education they might provide.

Young students who call themselves members of the Muslim Brotherhood, *Hizb ut-Tahrir* (the Party of Liberation), or Wahhabis are fierce rivals to this generation of imams. The young students run associations that organize Arabic lessons, tutoring and religious instruction. Sometimes they even work from the inside, at first assisting the imams, and gradually taking over the role of educator for children and young people. These young students thus manage to be in contact with the young members of the second generation of immigrants. Hitherto, serious and moderate traditional religious instruction has been almost nonexistent.

Certain authors come up again and again: Sayyid Qutb, Abul Ala Mawdudi, Yusuf Al-Qaradawi, Muhammad ibn Abd Al-Wahhab, Ibn Baz, 'Abd ul-Aziz Al-Uthaymeen – all leading figures of Wahhabism and the Muslim Brotherhood, also known as Qutbists. What do they write? One or two selected excerpts from Sayyid Qutb (1906–1996) may be instructive:

> Today, a Muslim society no longer exists, there is no more Islam and there are no more Muslims ... Muslim society will only come back into being when existing regimes have been destroyed, and given way to a power which respects divine legislation to the letter ... All the societies in the world, with no exceptions, are idolatrous and full of infidels, conscious that authority belongs solely to God. For when a man dares to invent laws, he proclaims himself the equal of God. And all peoples which subject themselves to such a man without resistance or rebellion are in a state of adoration of him, by their obedience to him [...]. The true Muslim today is the Muslim who makes *jihad* against all governments whose legislation is human in origin, in order to topple them and reinstate divine legislation.[23]

[23] Sayyid Qutb, *A l'ombre du Qour'an* (*In the Shade of the Koran*), Al-Hidayah Al-Islamiyah, 1988.

[...]

Hatred oozes from every page. These statements are the manifestation of an embittered and even sectarian state of mind, and they are accordingly dangerous.

[...]

It is undeniable that Wahhabi and Qutbist ideologies lie at the root of numerous murders, assassinations, attacks, massacres, and many civil wars. In the recent past, with the birth of Wahhabism, there have been massacres at Mecca, Medina, and Ta'if, as well as in Jordon, Iraq, Kuwait, and the United Arab Emirates.

[...]

It is important to lend an ear to Muslims following the instruction of the four traditional Sunni schools: Malikite, Shafite, Hanafite, and Hanbalite. These Muslims, backed up by arguments and proof, unveil the falsehoods of Wahhabis and Qutbists. To gain an ear within the Muslim community, these latter cultivate the illusion of truth and do their utmost to give the appearance of religious legality. They also use terms which have powerful positive connotations within the Muslim community, for example Muslim Brotherhood and Salafites. Their use of such terms is improper and unjustified, an usurpation with the aim to lead the neophyte astray. This is why it is crucial that the representatives of Sunni Islam wage a determined intellectual struggle. It would be suicidal for our society to sideline those who are the first line of defense against extremism and fanaticism.

Source: Abd Samad Moussaoui, Zacarias, My Brother: The Making of a Terrorist *(New York: Seven Stories Press, 2003), 49–54, 55, 56, 60.*

EXERCISE

What reasons does the author give for the attraction of Wahhabi groups to young French-Algerian Muslims, and why does he reject their position himself?

DISCUSSION

In the first part of the reading Moussaoui shows how he and his brother were denied access to their Muslim and Arabic heritage by their mother, and they felt too embarrassed to ask their North African friends about it. He argues that religious ignorance is important in understanding the appeal of Wahhabi groups. Arab-Muslim bookshops, which stock Wahhabi material, are more culturally accessible than mainstream bookshops, and the material is pitched at a less intellectual and affluent readership. Those entrusted with teaching Islam are often only qualified in Arabic language and rote-learning of the Qur'an, lacking theological and political education. In contrast, the more extremist position is often presented more attractively and accessibly.

While in prison, Sayyid Qutb, an influential member of the Muslim Brotherhood who was imprisoned in the 1950s and eventually executed by the Egyptian government in 1966, adopted the Wahhabis position that lapsed Muslims should not be considered true Muslims. From this position he went on to justify armed resistance to Muslim regimes deemed corrupt. Qutb is discussed further later in this section, but we should note here that his view is rejected by many followers of the Muslim Brotherhood today, although it remains influential for some, including among some Wahhabi and related groups. A passage from Qutb illustrating this insurrectionist position is quoted in the reading. Moussaoui rejects this position because it contradicts the main Islamic legal authorities, who all hold that if a ruler is a Muslim (defined simply in terms of declaring the *shahada*), then he or she cannot justly be removed by force. □

The following contrasting extracts reflect different aspects of the struggle to develop non-violent politics in Islam: on the one hand, a strong tradition running back to the earliest sources and practice of Muhammad of toleration and recognition of human, cultural and religious diversity; on the other hand, traditions of intolerance and the conditions of violence and oppression in which many contemporary Muslim communities find themselves. Reading 13 lays out some of the sources for recognition of the legitimacy of pluralism in all spheres of life in Islam, while acknowledging intolerant strands; Reading 14 tells a short story of non-violence in action in the context of the first Palestinian uprising (*intifada*) against Israel.

Pluralism and diversity

READING 13

Pluralism and diversity are among the core values of the Islamic religious and cultural tradition. The Qur'an recognizes diversity and tolerance of differences based on gender (49:13; 53:45), skin color, language (30:23), belief, and rank (64:2, 6:165). Harmony between the different social groupings and communities is praised, and competition and control of one by the other is condemned (2:213, 10:19, 7:38, 13:30, 16:63, 29:18, 35:42, 41:42, 64:18). The Qur'an asserts that differences are inherent in human life and part of God's plan for humanity. Thus ethnic, tribal, and national differences have no real bearing on closeness to God. The extent and degree of faith is the sole criterion by which different groups will be judged. The existence of difference among people is a basic assumption in Islam. Scholars cite the Prophet's saying, 'My Ummah's differences are a mercy' [...].

To protect such diversity among people, the Qur'an repeatedly emphasizes the respect and protection of People of the Book, and the Prophet stressed that 'on the day of Judgment I myself will act as the accuser of any person who oppresses a person under protection (*dhimma*) of Islam, and lays excessive [financial or other social] burdens on him' [...] The Prophet also supported of the unity and harmony of Islam with other religions: 'We the prophets are brothers and our religions are one and the same' [...].

Thus, differences among people are an inevitable and integral feature of humanity. 'If thy Lord had so willed, He could have made mankind one People: But they will not cease to dispute' (11:118). These differences are integrally related to the free will that God has bestowed on humanity, for people should be expected to be diverse not only in nationality and affiliation, but also in the expression of their faith and the path that they choose to follow (also see Qur'an, 10:99). Such a principle of free will and an individual's responsibility for all his or her actions is reflected in the Qur'an: 'If Allah so willed, He could make you all one People: but He leaves straying whom He pleases, and He guides whom He pleases: but ye shall certainly be called to account for all your actions' (16:93).

Tolerance of the 'other,' or non-Muslim, believers (People of the Book) is repeatedly accepted and emphasized in Islam. The equality of the followers of different religions is reiterated in both the Qur'an and Hadith. Muslims are asked to remember that there is no difference in the treatment of people of different religions except in their faith and deeds (3:113–14, 2:62, 5:68). The Qur'an calls on Muslims to abandon fighting and to coexist peacefully with people of other religions. It reaffirms the validity of the traditions of other faiths and requires its followers to respect their scriptures. In fact, the expansion of Islam through al-da'awah in Asia and Africa or the Pacific region took place mainly among non-Muslims. Under such circumstances Islam could not have survived or prospered without having been strongly pluralistic and tolerant of diversity [...].

There are many Qur'anic verses supporting this strong notion of pluralism in Islam. Some of these verses follow:

> Say, 'O People of the Book! Come to common terms as between us and you: that we worship none but Allah; that we associate no partners with Him; that we erect not, from among ourselves, lords and patrons other than Allah.' If then they turn their back, say ye: 'Bear witness that we (at least) are Muslims (bowing to Allah's Will).' (3:64)

> Say, 'O People of the Book, you have no ground to stand upon unless you stand fast by the Torah and the Bible and all that has been revealed to you from your Lord. ... Those who believe (in the Qur'an), those who follow the Jewish scriptures and Sabians and the Christians – any people who believe in God, the Day of Judgment, and do good deeds, on them shall be no fear nor shall they grieve.' (5:68–69)

Pluralism prevailed in the early Muslim community. There was no single Islamic law or constitution, no standardization of the Islamic law. The Sunni tradition yielded four legitimate schools of thought, none of which were limited to purely legal precepts (Esack 1998). In fact, the Qur'an is used to legitimize the validity of difference (*ikhtilaf*). Several interpretations of the Qur'an coexisted simultaneously in several areas. On the other hand, Islam has been intolerant of unbelievers, or infidels (*kafir*; pl. *kuffar*). Throughout history those who were cast as infidels were persecuted and punished by rulers and other followers.

The Medina charter, which was contracted between the Prophet and the various tribes, is an example of the high level of tolerance and respect of diversity assumed by Islam. Under the charter, all Muslims and Jewish tribes (apparently, no Christians were involved at that time, but it was used as a guiding principle in dealing with Christian tribes later) are considered one community, but each tribe retains its identity, customs, and internal relations. The charter was supplemented by a set of rules derived from the Qur'an and Sunnah to protect the rights of each group. Freedom of religion and the right not to be guilty because of the deed of an ally were among the protected rights.

Pluralism in Islam is reflected in the belief that the people are one community (Ummah), bound by a moral and spiritual identity and not by any other categories (such as race, birth, or gender). Sachedina even goes further, rejecting a narrow interpretation of the Qur'an verses that suggest salvation to Muslims only. He refutes the notion that the principle of 'only my religion is genuine' exists in the Qur'an or the belief that only Islam rests on truths received in revelation, only Islam possesses the intrinsic values necessary for attaining religious perfection. In refuting these three principles of antipluralism he reinterprets the Qur'an verses that historically have been used to support such principles [...]. For example, he explains that when commentators and interpreters explain the term Islam they restrict it to the Muslim community instead of explaining it as an act of surrender and submission to God, usually including all the *mu'ahidin* (people who believe in one God and are in peaceful relations with Muslims). Another example of change in interpretation is the use of the term *unbeliever*. Historically it referred to the pagan Arabs, whom the Muslim attempted to convert. However, with time, interpreters began expanding the term to include Christians and Jews. This tendency contradicts both the Prophet's teachings and the Qur'an's equal recognition of the People of the Book.

The Qur'an emphasizes repeatedly that 'humankind is one community.' Among the principles Sachedina (2000, 23–25) identifies as the basis for religious pluralism in Islam are: (1) the unity of humankind under one God; (2) the particularity of religions brought by the prophets; and (3) the role of revelation (the Qur'an). As Sachedina asserts, these principles do not deny the contradictions that might exist among religions, and they recognize the oneness of humanity and the need to work for better understanding among people of faith. The notion of freedom of conscience in matters of faith is the cornerstone of the Qur'an's notion of religious pluralism, both at the interreligious and intrareligious levels. Such principles constitute a strong base for Islamic approaches to interfaith dialogue and understanding.

Source: Mohammed Abu-Nimer, Nonviolence and Peacebuilding in Islam: Theory and Practice *(Gainesville, Florida: University of Florida Press, 2003), 78–80, references omitted.*

EXERCISE

Why does Abu-Nimer argue that pluralism and diversity are core values in Islamic tradition?

DISCUSSION

Abu-Nimer argues that the Qur'an and *hadith* demonstrate that human diversity, including religious diversity and diversity of peoples, is part of God's plan. The Charter of Medina, in particular, provides an example of religious coexistence. Some scholars such as Sachedina (2000) go further, and argue that early Islam recognised salvation as extending to all monotheists at peace with the Muslim community. He also argues that freedom of conscience is a basic principle of Islam. □

READING 14

Nonviolence in Palestine

In February 1989, in the West Bank city of Hebron, an Israeli patrol was chasing a group of *shabab* (Palestinian youth, ten to twenty years old, who were in the forefront of the street protests) after a stone-throwing incident. In the course of the chase, a young protestor was shot and killed. As the chase continued, an Israeli soldier was cut off from the patrol and found himself surrounded by a group of angry shabab. Fearing for his life, he ran to the door of the nearest house and began beating on it with his rifle. A woman came and opened the door and, seeing the danger, admitted him to the house and refused to let the shabab enter and attack him. With the shabab milling around outside, she served the soldier coffee and waited for the mob to disperse so he could leave safely. The woman was the mother of the boy whom the patrol had just killed.

About a month later, in the course of a conversation in Hebron about nonviolence in the Intifada, the researcher asked a group of Palestinians what role religion played in their struggle. Ahmad, the host, replied, 'Religion and custom enable us to preserve our humanity.' When asked to elaborate, he told the above story and added, 'This is why nonviolence is important to us. We will never become like the Israelis and hate our enemy; we will offer him hospitality. That soldier could come back again and the woman would offer him coffee again.' The family and friends sitting in the room nodded their assent to the story and the discussion.

This story illustrates several issues. First, it is a microcosm of the complex intertwining of violence and nonviolence that characterizes the Intifada and calls into question simple distinctions between the two. The shabab provoked the action by throwing stones, prompting the soldiers' fatal gunfire. One soldier's fearful response to potential violence resulted in nonviolent protection by the woman. By sorting out the complexities of these types of action and their interaction in the Intifada, perhaps we can further our understanding of how nonviolent resistance functions in movements of social protest. Second, the story hints at ways that Islam functions in relation to nonviolence. When asked about religion, Ahmad linked it with custom and proceeded to tell a story rather than turning to theory, theology, or narrowly defined religion. Therefore, exploring religion in its social context may help us understand the subtle interaction of religion and nonviolence in the Intifada.

Third, the story illustrates a particular way of talking about nonviolence. It does not recall a grand action of heroism or focus on a charismatic leader or deal in theological or ideological abstractions. It neither offers a database for sociological analysis nor develops systemic theories. But the anecdotal evidence it offers of the way that Palestinians were thinking and acting in a very real, very nasty struggle compels us to take it seriously. The model it presents of one family's attitudes and actions in the Intifada gives the moral and theoretical dimension and introduces potentially different avenues of approach to analyzing movements of social protest and the role of nonviolence in such movements.

Source: Mohammed Abu-Nimer and Joe Groves, 'Peacebuilding and nonviolent political movements in Arab-Muslim communities', in Mohammed Abu-Nimer, Nonviolence and Peacebuilding in Islam *(Gainesville, Florida: University of Florida Press), 128–9.*

EXERCISE

What values are demonstrated in this story, and how might they help in peace building?

DISCUSSION

Religion and custom are seen by the teller of the story as the basis for preserving Palestinians' humanity in the face of Israeli oppression. This humanity is shown in the woman taking pity on the Israeli soldier, recognising him as a fellow human being in need, in spite of the conflict they are both part of. Hospitality is also a religiously and culturally rooted way of expressing that common humanity. The strength of determination not to dehumanise the enemy is shown particularly strikingly in the storyteller's assertion that the woman would do the same even if she knew that the soldier had shot her son. This, it might be argued, is precisely the opposite of the Kharijite/Wahhabi exclusion of other Muslims from the fold of true believers; instead of restricting the moral universe to allow harm of those excluded, the story insists on seeing the enemy as one to whom a duty of hospitality is owed. □

The 'greater *jihad*'

Read Ruthven, 'The greater *jihad*' and 'The Sufi *tariqas*', on pages 128 to 132.

EXERCISE

What is the 'greater *jihad*', and how did the Sufi *tariqas* help to spread it?

DISCUSSION

According to a *hadith* of the Prophet, the 'greater *jihad*' is the struggle against evil, which affects all aspects of a Muslim's personal and social life. After the early military conquests, Islam spread throughout the early medieval period primarily through trade, to China as early as the ninth century, then to southern Africa, India and South-East Asia. Although there were no formal missionary organisations, many merchants were members of Sufi *tariqas*, which we first came across in Reading 9. These brotherhoods each followed a particular *tariqa* or path traced back through a line of teachers to the Prophet, his companions or the founders of the various groups. Bound by common spiritual disciplines and a tradition of esoteric teachings, the *tariqas* became a formidable social and even political influence in many Muslim societies. □

Read Ruthven, '*Jihad* and resistance' and 'Reformers and modernists', on pages 133 to 135.

EXERCISE

Why did the 'lesser *jihad*' come to the fore again in response to European expansion, and how did reformists and modernists differ in their responses to modernity?

DISCUSSION

The 'lesser *jihad*' – war – came to the fore in the nineteenth century as predominantly European powers began to encroach on *dar al-Islam*. Such movements were often led by members of Sufi orders, and include the rebellion led by Prince Dipanegara against the Dutch in Java (1825–30), by Barelwi among the Pathans (Pashtuns) against the British on India's north-west frontier (1826–1831), by the Chechen leader Shamil against the Russians in the Caucasus (1834–59), but also against the Egyptians and the British by Muhammad ibn 'Abdullah in Sudan.

Reformists stressed religious reform within the tradition, adopted some modern ideas (such as stressing individual responsibility), and often adopted modern communication techniques such as printing, post and rail. However, their non-elite social status meant that they were not in a position to implement more fundamental change. An example is the Deobandi movement, which spread from the college of Deoband in northern India, founded in 1867.

In contrast, modernists were more likely to be from indigenous elites and thus most intensively exposed to European influences and least subject to social constraints. Hence they frequently adopted European dress, military techniques, methods of production, administration and education. Such reform was not just attempted under colonial rule: Ottoman rulers in Egypt and elsewhere attempted all these reforms. Sayyid Ahmed Khan was one of the most radical modernists because he attempted to modernise Qur'anic hermeneutics, as well as teaching English-style education (and English language) alongside a more traditional Islamic syllabus at his elite Muhammadan Anglo-Oriental College in Aligarh, India. Khan was one of the first to make the characteristic modernist distinction between the details of revelation (*furu*), which he saw as historically contingent, and underlying principles (*usul*).

Although he regarded the truth of the Qur'anic revelation as final, he saw the rest of the tradition as open to question and reinterpretation. □

Read Ruthven, 'The end of the caliphate', 'The quest for an Islamic state', 'The Muslim Brotherhood', 'The new *jahiliya*', 'The impact of the Iranian revolution' and 'The appeal of Islamism', pages 137 to 146.

EXERCISE

How have Muslims responded to the end of the caliphate, and how and why has the idea of an Islamic state come to be seen as an attractive political solution for many in Muslim-majority societies?

DISCUSSION

The abolition of the caliphate by Mustafa Kemal's Turkish nationalists in 1924 made incontrovertible what had been clear for a long time: that the authority of the Ottoman caliph had become a fiction. No one outside the empire had supported the caliph's call for *jihad* in 1914, and his empire was dismembered in part by British-inspired Arab rebellions. An attempt to revive the caliphal ideal in India met with no external support, and the energies of supporters of this idea were eventually directed towards the creation of an Islamic republic in Pakistan. In Egypt, the 1920s saw Muslim intellectuals busy trying to formulate a post-caliphal model of Islamic political legitimacy, using the same principles of *shura* (consultation), judicial authority and the revival of *shari'a* that have subsequently characterised discussions of the 'Islamic state'.

Hasan al-Banna, an Egyptian school teacher, founded the Muslim Brotherhood in 1928 to encourage Islamic revival from the grassroots. Al-Banna was highly critical of Western culture, and his rhetoric has had a continuing influence on Islamist movements (boxed text on pages 142 and 143). Furthermore, political experience radicalised the group – especially the crisis for Arabs in Palestine from the 1930s culminating in *al-nakhba* ('the disaster') of mass displacement in the Israeli war of independence (1947–49). Although the Brotherhood supported the overthrow of the monarchy in 1952 that led to the rule of Nasser and his 'Free Officers', like other potential sources of opposition they were soon suppressed, and further radicalised.

After al-Banna's assassination in 1949, Sayyid Qutb (1906–66), whose writings were quoted in the extract from Moussaoui (2003; Reading 12), rose to prominence. Once an employee in the Ministry of Education, Qutb was imprisoned for most of the 1950s and 60s, and finally hanged for plotting to assassinate Nasser. Qutb's time in jail served the Islamist cause well in the long run however, for while there he wrote some of the movement's most influential works, including a monumental thirty-volume Qur'anic commentary and, perhaps most influentially of all, *Milestones* or *Signposts* (see Ruthven, the boxed text on pages 144 to 145). Qutb rejected al-Banna's idea that Islamisation can occur purely from below. Rather, action at the level of the state is required, and this means revolution. To support this, Qutb made the same powerful ideological move as the Wahhabists, which was to break with Sunni tradition's acceptance that all who declare the *shahada* are indeed Muslims, and argued that unless they live by *shari'a* they must be judged unbelievers, against whom *jihad* is obligatory. Like the Wahhabis, he also saw contemporary Muslim societies as *jahiliya* in need of cleansing.

The ideas of such Islamist thinkers received a considerable boost from the Iranian revolution of 1979. Although in a distinctive Shi'ite tradition, figures such as Khomeini and especially 'Ali Sharia'ti represented the kind of synthesis of modern Western thought turned into a radical critique of Western civilisation. In particular, Sharia'ti drew extensively on Marxist, existentialist and anti-colonialist elements in Western thought. Both Khomeini and Sharia'ti advocated an Islamic state under *shari'a* of a kind similar to that which Sunni Islamists advocate. Yet little direct activity among Sunnis was stimulated.

Ruthven's argument in the section on 'The appeal of Islamism' is that such a radical doctrine has appealed increasingly widely to people disillusioned with the economic and political failure of their nationalist governments and frustrated that their educational achievements have not led to more material progress. However, here it is important to recall the discussion of similar ideas in the section 'Alternative views of the social bases of Islamism' which expressed scepticism concerning attempts to identify simply materialist causes for Islamist revival. Two reasons for this were the poor fit between the socio-economic groups that should most espouse Islamist ideologies according to such theories, and the reality of the widespread appeal of the movement. It may be better to see the spread of Islamic private voluntary organisations in Egypt and elsewhere rather as the 'missing civil society', whose absence Ruthven, following the sociologist Ernest Gellner (1994), and ultimately Marx and Weber, sees as a cause of political and economic stagnation in Muslim-majority societies (for an alternative view see Turner, 1994, or Herbert, 2003, Chapter 3). Thus the growth of Islamic private voluntary organisations may be seen as a sign of the reinvigoration of society, which could lead in a variety of directions, including economic development and political reform. □

11
Islam and Islamism: the future?

Read Ruthven, 'Urbanization and its effects', 'The international dimension', 'The problem of modernization', 'The future of Islamism' on pages 146 to 157.

EXERCISE

1 What trends in contemporary Islam does Ruthven discuss in this section?

2 How does Ruthven see Islam developing in the future?

DISCUSSION

1 Among the trends that Ruthven refers to on pages 146–7 is, firstly, the increase in religious observance mentioned earlier in the set book (2012, 21–2). This he regards as a kind of cultural defence mechanism helping migrants from the countryside to deal with the challenges they face in urban areas. On pages 151–2 he elaborates on this by describing the various aspects of social change and dislocation driving this defensive reaction. However, you should note – as was observed in the section 'Alternative views on the social bases of Islamism' – that some scholars (e.g. Starrett, 1998) have cast doubt on this theory, in Starrett's case in relation to Egypt.

Secondly, Ruthven refers to the growing social role of Islamic welfare organisations and charitable associations, and the way that they address problems resulting from governments' failure to address the difficulties caused by rapid urbanization and the growth of slums and shanty-towns (2012, 146–7). In this connection on pages 156 and 157 he looks at the way the Ismai'li community led by the Aga Khan has been able to address concerns for welfare and social justice, as well as discussing the Gulen movement based in Turkey, which has particularly focused on education and 'constructive dialogue with religionists and humanists'. In this connection it is worth noting that although Ruthven cites Zubaida to the effect that Islamic groups apparently do not encourage 'popular participation' (147), some studies have suggested otherwise (e.g. Wickham, 1997, and Abdo, 2000, on Egypt; Hefner, 2000, on Indonesia).

Thirdly, on page 150 Ruthven draws attention to the growing restrictions on the rights of women and religious minorities that have resulted from the recent tendency for more traditionalist attitudes to replace modernist interpretations (some scholars have disagreed with him here as well) (Karam, 1998; Roald, 2001). Ruthven also refers here to conflicts between Muslims and members of other religious traditions, as well as to the significant increase in Sunni-Shi'a tensions, for example in Iraq and Pakistan (151–2).

Fourthly, Ruthven mentions the 'Facebook Revolution', pointing out that the 'Arab Spring' of 2011 for example does not seem to have been influenced to any great extent by specifically Islamic ideas. However, he sees the web and social media as contributing to 'the democratization of religiosity', undermining the authority of the religious scholars (*'ulama*), and facilitating the expression of a whole range of points of view by laymen and women, on a raft of controversial issues, political (for example mistreatment of Palestinians by Israeli settlers) and social (for instance homosexuality). Moreover the internet is contributing, Ruthven suggests, to the growth of a 'cyber-umma', helping to create a global community of like-minded Muslims, one that is transcending particular family, national, linguistic or ethnic identities. One expression of this is the proliferation of websites giving details of potential Muslim marriage-partners. Another is the way that it enables images of oppression and violence inflicted on Muslims to be widely circulated, and so attracts would-be jihadists. As Gary Bunt points out, 'without the Internet and its associated tools' Al-Qaeda would not have been able to function as it did (quoted in Ruthven, 2010, 154).

Finally, although he emphasizes the resilience of the territorial state in the Muslim-majority world, on page 152 Ruthven emphasizes that Islamism seems 'set to remain a significant political factor in Muslim lands for the foreseeable future'. He also refers to some militant Islamic movements, including transnational ones like Al-Qaeda, and territorially-based ones, in particular the Taliban in Afghanistan and Pakistan (150). Though he doesn't mention them here, we might also note the presence of comparable movements in Yemen and Somalia. He also draws attention to 'local conflicts arising from the position of Muslim majorities living under non-Muslim governments', and explains that these can take the form of 'jihads', for instance in Kashmir and Chechnya (2010, 152).

2 Ruthven thinks that social and political (i.e. exoteric) Islam are still dominant. Islamism will, he suggests, remain an important political influence in Muslim-majority countries for the foreseeable future, and concludes the book on rather a pessimistic note. However, he suggests that, as has happened with Christianity in the West, thanks to the 'processes of historical and technological change', Islam will gradually become more private and voluntary. His view is therefore that in the

longer term 'more quietist versions of Islam' – pietistic and mystical traditions – are likely to gain ground.

An alternative perspective on Islamic/Islamist futures

Anthony Shadid was an American political journalist of Arab background who travelled across the Middle East in 1999–2000 in an attempt to understand his own origins and the societies there. The epilogue reproduced here was published with the second edition of the book, and was written in response to the events of September 11th, 2001.

READING 15

The legacy of the Prophet

in the introduction to *Legacy of the Prophet*, I suggested that researching and writing the book, on one level, constituted a personal journey for me. In the United States, I had felt the disenchantment and, at times, resentment that so many hyphenated Americans of Middle East origin do: Stereotypes and prejudices against Arabs and Muslims always seemed to hit home. Yet I was often as puzzled by those same two identities – the Arab world from which my ancestors came and the religion, Islam, which shapes and defines that world's cultures, traditions, politics and memories, for Christians, Muslims and Jews alike. Those questions and conflicts made the book, in the beginning, a search for my own identity, potentially providing answers about my relationship to both my country of birth and the place of my ancestors.

As I look back on the turbulence, confusion and anger since the events of September 11, I have a different sense of that search. Reflecting on my interviews and conversations, my research and travels, I feel that my fractured identity has, in fact, given me a small chance to see the long-standing conflict between East and West in a different light. To many, a generation after the Iranian Revolution, the shot heard around the Muslim world, the sense of animosity and enmity between the two persists unabated, deepened dangerously by the attacks on New York and Washington. Islam, at least in the West, comes across as unyielding, blinded by its anger and inspired by vengeance. Many Muslims see the West as equally inflexible. Both seem short on understanding. Yet by default and through luck of birth and circumstance, I spent much of my time in the Middle East outside that relationship that was loosely 'us' versus 'them.' I typically fell into a gray area, comfortable with neither but, as a journalist, interested in both. At times consciously, more often not, I tried to step outside the traditional equation. In hindsight, I was looking for the alternatives to what we have come to believe as truths – that Islam is one way, the West another and that religion can represent one immutable standard.

The years I spent in the Middle East represent a turning point in the region's history. Broadly, both faith and politics are changing. Far removed from the *jihad* of Osama bin Ladin, their relationship to each other is being reinterpreted, and many of the people whose lives are guided by them are asking bold, far-reaching questions that, in time, will have to be answered. In day-to-day life, Islamic political movements are using the faith and its appeal to Muslims' roots and identity, powerful forces in an uncertain world, to frame their political, social and economic programs. The goal is to create an alternative in a landscape colored by despotism and repression and gripped by war and a perceived clash of cultures. Although each locale has its own specific conditions – one of Islam's strengths, of course, is its adaptability – essential ideas are being shared: democracy, the right to religious interpretation, the role of religion in politics and notion of *umma*.

Umma, perhaps, is the most powerful of those ideas. The Islamic concept of community and people seemed to play a permanent role in the lives of the individuals I met, from soldiers to activists to scholars. Mirza Khan, on the lonely plains of Afghanistan, found in it a mission. Eid Rabia, the trashman in Cairo, found security. To him, *umma* meant the community of Muslims, of Egyptians, of Cairenes, of the group of men who spent time with him in a café drinking tea sweetened just right. In it was his answer to Cairo's bewildering, mystifying changes, a language of resistance and, as important, his moral reference. In a way, I thought, it was his utopia of mind.

[...]

The rhetoric and exploits of wandering militants like bin Ladin, while appealing to a small segment of a Muslim world disenchanted to the point of hopelessness, rings hollow to the overwhelming majority. The realities of war and the promises of revolution are distant – both in physical terms and in the sense of their relevance. The real force of Islamic politics is represented by movements that have incorporated the new currents of thought with the persuasive and successful application of *da'wa*, an Islamic brand of welfare and social activism. These movements can be in opposition, as with Hamas in Palestine, or a complement to those in power, as with Hezbollah in Lebanon. In their most mature form, they can take on the visage of electoral politics, as with Islamists in Turkey. At the level of the polity itself, though, the effect of these movements, across the region, is remarkably uniform: In all cases they engage the general population, not in seeking intangible goals in some far-off future but in making a better life in the here and now – at the local level, where *umma* can be felt, seen, and even *used* profoundly.

[...]

Yet although the shape and pace of politics in individual countries may diverge, one can still point to a general trend across the Islamic political spectrum. Many states share a history of colonialism as well as postcolonial disappointment as succeeding governments were no more just or democratic than their imperial predecessors. Typically, those governments are best remembered for their failures: the 1967 war, Stalinist-style repression and economies that ridicule promises of prosperity. The most vibrant response today to that disappointment comes in the form of politicized religion as it is taken up by Islamic intellectuals, movements like Hezbollah and the Center Party in Egypt, political parties such as the Islamic Action Front in Jordan and even governments in the throes of change like Iran under President Mohammad Khatami. Together, they have broadly abandoned tradition to help reform the faith, giving it a legitimate role – both practically and potentially – in the political life of their countries. These currents share their belief in Islam as the framework of action, looking to religion in one way or another to address their social, political and economic concerns. More often than not, they are the ones most likely to draw the broadest support from a public resentful over inequities, injustice, chronic weakness and the slavish imitation of the West by indigenous elites. These movements see in Islam and its resonant symbols their legitimacy; they see in its non-Western concepts – *umma*, for instance – an alternative, independent rationale and framework for an Islamic polity. And across the region, they see within the faith a justification for a democratic, progressive region that is currently neither. All of them appeal to Islam as an overarching institution and ideology, even if their specific goals and programs are diverse and, at times, contradictory.

Will these movements find success? Yes, but gradually. In coming years, many of the governments in the Middle East – Egypt, Palestine, Turkey and countries in much of North Africa among them – will be forced to compromise with the Islamist elements in their midst. Simply put, the groups command too much popular support and represent too important a political current to be indefinitely neglected or, even worse, repressed. The alternative is insecurity and instability, the dread of all authoritarian governments. The survival of these governments will require a degree of transparency – and the reform that requires – if they are to engage economically and politically with the rest of the world. In a landscape without superpower rivalry and knit tighter together, for better or worse, by a neoliberal vision of the future, bureaucratic authoritarianism will in time prove less acceptable, even if in the short term it finds its repression sanctioned under the pretext of the emergency that followed the events of September 11. Through that inevitable future, I believe a window of opportunity will open, however slightly, making possible a compromise between the states and their Islamist opposition.

Although I admit being less certain than when I finished the book in 2000, I still remain hopeful for this scenario. My reason is this: I suspect that the future Middle East – in terms of its relationship between Islam and the state – will eventually witness a degree of the political transformation that Western Europe underwent during the twentieth century. There, Soviet-style socialism underwent a long metamorphosis to the social democracy of today. It was both a tactical and an ideological shift, dictated to a large extent by political survival. The parties and currents of the left were incorporated into the European political system without threatening its survival. Eventually, through political necessity, the same will go for Islamic parties. Already, a coming moderation on the part of Islamists is evident in the departure of the Center Party from the Muslim Brotherhood, President Khatami from his revolutionary antecedents and the Virtue Party in Turkey from its more militant predecessors. The changes reflect a broader trend toward integration rather than the past practice of offering an alternative.

Source: Anthony Shadid, Legacy of the Prophet *(Boulder, Colorado: Westview Press, 2002), 289–93.*

EXERCISE

How does Shadid see the future of Islamic political movements, and how does his vision of Islamic futures converge with and diverge from Ruthven's?

DISCUSSION

Shadid sees a tendency towards democracy in these movements which makes them quite distinct from 'top-down' Islamism, and able to engage popular participation effectively. In spite of September 11th, 2001, he sees governments in Muslim-majority societies as likely to come to an accommodation gradually with their Islamist movements that will increase openness and democracy in those societies. Thus his vision diverges from Ruthven's, because he sees a future for a communally oriented faith based on ideas of *umma*, rather than a privatised Islam. However, his view converges with Ruthven in the sense that individual choice also develops in his scenario, but as a result of greater freedom and democracy rather than privatisation. Thus Islam becomes more a matter of personal choice, but also of collective responsibility.

It is worth looking back to the attitudes to Islam's public role demonstrated in the study by Hassan (2002) discussed earlier (see Reading 3). With the high levels of religious observance, close connections perceived between religious orthodoxy and political security, and high public trust in religious leaders demonstrated in Egypt, Indonesia and Pakistan in this study, it is difficult to see how Islam could become significantly privatised in Muslim-majority societies in the foreseeable future. □

Conclusion

To conclude, we shall consider two different perspectives: one personal and from a Muslim, the other academic and from a non-Muslim, on the challenges facing contemporary Islam. First the thoughts of the British-born, Pakistani-heritage Muslim, Monawar Hussein, who is interviewed on Audio CD 1, tracks 35 to 41. At the time of recording (February 2005), Hussein was training to be an imam at the Muslim College in Ealing, on a course specifically designed to meet the needs of imams to serve Muslim communities in Britain, although students also come to study from across the world. Hussein had also recently been appointed as the first Muslim chaplain at Eton College, the well-known public school for boys.

EXERCISE

Listen to the interview with Monawar Hussein on Audio CD 1, tracks 35 to 41 and consider the following questions:

1 What relationship does Hussein see between his previous life in business and his faith?

2 What difficulties with the training of imams did the course at the Muslim College seek to address?

3 How did Hussein's friends and family react to his decision to become an imam?

4 What does Hussein see as the challenges and opportunities facing the Muslim community over the next decade?

DISCUSSION

1 Hussein sees no barriers between the two: integrity is as vital in his business life as in his life as an imam.

2 Many imams have either been trained on the Indian subcontinent or use training methods little changed from that context, so they may lack skills – such as fluency in English language – to enable them to communicate with the communities they serve. The course seeks to address these issues by providing pastoral and practical training relevant to the UK context, as well as training in Islamic traditions.

3 Some have found Hussein's decision strange, as most of his contemporaries have focused on better-paid careers, such as jobs in IT and management.

4 Speaking from his personal experience of involvement with the new mosque in Oxford, Hussein believes it is important for the Muslim community to open its doors to non-Muslims, so that they feel welcome and find out what the Muslim community is about. This may be seen as an example of the pluralistic Islam that Ruthven envisages in his conclusion. □

It will be useful now for you to listen again to the interview with Ruthven on Audio CD 1, tracks 25 to 34 and to refer back to the answers you gave at the beginning of this study guide after you had first listened to the interview.

EXERCISE

Now consider the following questions. (You may find it useful to pause to refer back to places in the study guide or Ruthven (2012) where the issues are discussed.)

1 What does Ruthven see as the main factors and developments shaping contemporary Islam?

2 Why does Ruthven see rural–urban migration as a key factor in contemporary Muslim experience?

3 Where does Ruthven see clues to the future of Islam?

DISCUSSION

1 Many factors are discussed. Ruthven sees religious nationalist movements as significant, but ultimately likely to be eclipsed by a pluralist version of Islam compatible with personal choice in religion and modern consumer lifestyles. Other factors include the impact of modernisation, including industrialisation, rural–urban migration (nationally and internationally), the growth in electronic communication (especially of visual culture), the organisational flexibility and durability of Sufism, and its spiritual appeal.

2 Rural–urban migration (national and transnational) is important because: (a) it is such a widespread experience for contemporary Muslims; (b) it presents profound challenges to forms of religion closely associated for generations with rural ways of life; (c) it tends to force people to choose between secularism and a more self-conscious and assertive form of religion, often strongly linked with identity.

3 Ruthven sees clues to the future of Islam in Muslim minorities in the West and South-East Asia, especially Indonesia and Malaysia. Muslims in the West are a kind of vanguard in terms of finding practical adaptations to modern lifestyles, and have good access to global means of communication. But South-East Asia is important

> because, as they are Muslim-majority societies, changes emanating from there are much more difficult for traditionalists to resist as inauthentic or originating in the West. □

So, what are we to make of the rather different Islamic futures envisaged by Shadid, Ruthven and Hussein? It should be evident from this study that while it has a clear ritual, scriptural and (in many ways) ethical core, Islam is a very rich and diverse tradition. In view of this, it is not surprising that contemporary Muslims and other commentators addressing such a big question as how they see the future of Islam, are likely to come up with different answers.

Shadid travelled across the Middle East, and perhaps his experience reflects the situation there: his vision includes many repressive and struggling governments, faced by forms of Islamism which have gradually (in many cases) become more mainstream and less militant, though without losing militant forms altogether, especially in continued trouble spots.

Ruthven, in contrast, looks more towards South and South-East Asia, towards forms of Islam developing as minorities in Western societies, and to Sufism. Here the grasp of modernity (new technologies and economic opportunities) and accommodation with pluralism are more evident, and he presents Sufism as a form of Islam that is particularly adaptable, attracting both Western converts and providing an organisational structure for the transmission of Islam in a variety of contexts.

Hussein offers a more personal and domestic vision, stemming from his UK experience working in business, helping with building a new mosque, and training to become an imam. But his vision of openness and dialogue in a plural situation articulates well with the emerging trends discerned by Ruthven, and even (if more distantly) with more pluralist versions of Islamism found by Shadid across the Middle East.

If you have enjoyed this introduction to Islam and would like to learn more, when you have finished A217 you might like to consider continuing your study by taking a higher-level module.

Bibliography

Abbas, S. (2002) *The Female Voice in Sufi Ritual*, Austin, TX, University of Texas Press.

Abdo, E. (2000) *No God but God: Egypt and the Triumph of Islam*, Oxford, Oxford University Press.

Abu-Nimer, M. (2003) *Nonviolence and Peacebuilding in Islam: Theory and Practice*, Gainesville, Florida, University of Florida Press.

Akhtar, S. (1989) *Be Careful with Muhammad*, London, Bellew.

Alibhai, Y. (1989) 'Satanic betrayals', *New Statesman and Society*, 2 February, 12.

Baer, E. (2004) *The Human Figure in Islamic Art: Inheritances and Islamic Transformations*, Costa Mesa, CA, Mazda.

Bowman, M. (1994) 'Islam, adat and multiculturalism in Malaysia', *DISKUS* 2:1, 15–27.

El Guindi, F. (1999) *Veil: Modesty, Privacy and Resistance*, Oxford and New York, Berg.

Esack, F. (1994) *On Being a Muslim: Finding a Religious Path in the World Today*, Oxford, Oneworld.

Esposito, J.L. (1988) *Islam: The Straight Path*, Oxford, Oxford University Press.

Frishman, M. and Khan, H. (1994) *The Mosque: History, Architectural Development and Regional Diversity*, London, Thames and Hudson.

Gellner, E. (1994) *The Conditions of Liberty: Civil Society and its Enemies*, London, Penguin.

Gilsenan, M. (2000) *Recognising Islam: Religion and Society in the Modern Middle East*, London, IB Tauris.

Hassan, R. (2002) *Faithlines: Muslim Conceptions of Islam and Society*, Oxford, Oxford University Press.

Hefner, R. (2000) *Civil Islam: Muslims and Democratization in Indonesia*, Princeton, Princeton University Press.

Herbert, D. (2003) *Religion and Civil Society*, Aldershot, Ashgate.

Huntingdon, S. (1993) 'The clash of civilisations', *Foreign Affairs*, 72:3.

Kabbani, R. (1992) *Letter to Christendom*, London, Virago.

Karam, A. (1998) *Women, Islamisms and the State: Contemporary Feminisms in Egypt*, London, Macmillan.

King, R. (1999) *Orientalism and Religion*, London, Routledge.

Midgley, M. (1989) *Wisdom, Information and Wonder*, London, Routledge.

Moors, A. (2003) 'Islam and fashion on the streets of San'a, Yemen', *Etnofoor*, 16:2, 41–56.

Moussaoui, A.S. (2003) *Zacarias, My Brother: The Making of a Terrorist*, New York, Seven Stories Press.

Rippin, A. (1990) *Muslims: Their Religious Beliefs and Practices. Volume 1: The Formative Years*, London and New York, Routledge.

——— (1993) *Muslims: Their Religious Beliefs and Practices. Volume 2: The Contemporary Period*, London and New York, Routledge.

Roald, A.S. (2001) *Women in Islam: The Western Experience*, London and New York, Routledge.

Rushdie, S. (1988) *The Satanic Verses*, Harmondsworth, Penguin Viking.

Ruthven, M. (2012) *Islam: A Very Short Introduction*, 2nd edn, Oxford, Oxford University Press (set book).

Sachedina, A. (2000) *The Islamic Roots of Democratic Pluralism*, New York, Oxford University Press.

Said, E. (1997) *Covering Islam*, second edition, London, Vintage.

Shadid, A. (2002) *Legacy of the Prophet*, Boulder, CO, Westview Press.

Sherif, F. (1995) *A Guide to the Contents of the Qur'an*, Reading, Garnet.

Starrett, G. (1998) *Putting Islam to Work: Education, Politics and Religious Transformation in Egypt*, Berkeley, Los Angeles and London, University of California Press.

Therborn, G. (1997) 'Beyond civil society: democratic experiences and their relevance to the "Middle East"', in E. Özdalga and S. Persson (eds) *Civil Society and Democracy in the Muslim World*, Istanbul, Swedish Research Institute, 45–54.

Turner, B. (1994) *Orientalism, Postmodernism and Globalism*, London, Routledge.

Westwood, J. (ed.) (2003) *On Pilgrimage: Sacred Journeys around the World*, Mahwah, NJ, HiddenSpring.

Wickham, C. (1997) 'Islamic mobilization and political change: the Islamist trend in Egypt's political associations', in J. Stork and J. Benin (eds) *Political Islam: Essays from Middle East Report*, London, I.B. Tauris, 120–35.

Acknowledgements

My thanks to Marion Bowman for her work on the visual and material culture sections of the study guide, to Kate Clements for her patience in editing, and to Trinity College Dublin for allowing me time to complete this work for The Open University.

Grateful acknowledgement is made to the following sources for permission to reproduce material within this book.

Gÿlnar R. Baltanova, 'Mecca', in Jennifer Westwood (ed.) On Pilgrimage: Sacred Journeys around the World *(Mahwah, NJ: HiddenSpring, 2003), 8–10. HiddenSpring.*

Farid Esack, On Being a Muslim: Finding a Religious Path in the World Today *(Oxford: Oneworld, 1999), 12–17. Oneworld Publications.*

Riaz Hassan, Faithlines: Muslim Conceptions of Islam and Society *(Oxford: Oxford University Press, 2002). Copyright Oxford University Press, 2002. Reprinted with the permission of Oxford University Press, Pakistan from their publication entitled* Faithlines: Muslim Conceptions of Islam and Society *by Riaz Hassan.*

Farid Esack, On Being a Muslim: Finding a Religious Path in the World Today *(Oxford: Oneworld, 1999), 1–3. Oneworld Publications.*

'The Qur'an: The Word of God', 19–33, from Islam: The Straight Path, Third Edition, *by John L. Esposito, copyright 1998 by Oxford University Press, Inc. Used by permission of Oxford University Press, Inc.*

Shabbir Akhtar, Be Careful with Muhammad *(London: Bellew, 1989), vii, 1–3. Bellew Publishing Company Ltd. Used with permission of the author.*

Andrew Rippin, Muslims: Their Religious Beliefs and Practices *(London and New York: Routledge, 1993), 56–7, 59–61. Taylor and Francis.*

From The Female Voice in Sufi Ritual: Devotional Practices of Pakistan and India *by Shemeem Burney Abbas, foreword by Elizabeth Warnock Fernea, xiii–xv, 18–19, 25–7. Copyright © 2002. By permission of the University of Texas Press.*

Rana Kabbani, Letter to Christendom *(London: Virago, 1992), 22–8. Virago Press. Used with permission of the author.*

Anne Sofie Roald, Women in Islam: The Western Experience *(London and New York: Routledge, 2001), 145–6, 255, 267, 271–2. Taylor and Francis.*

Abd Samad Moussaoui, Zacarias, My Brother: The Making of a Terrorist *(New York: Seven Stories Press, 2003), 49–54, 55, 56, 60. Seven Stories Press.*

Mohammed Abu-Nimer, Nonviolence and Peacebuilding in Islam: Theory and Practice *(Gainesville: University Press of Florida, 2003), 78–80, references omitted. University Press of Florida.*

Mohammed Abu-Nimer and Joe Groves, 'Peacebuilding and nonviolent political movements in Arab-Muslim communities', in Mohammed Abu-Nimer, Nonviolence and Peacebuilding in Islam *(Gainesville: University Press of Florida, 2003), 128–9. University Press of Florida.*

Anthony Shadid, Legacy of the Prophet *(Boulder, CO: Westview Press, 2002), 289–93. Perseus Books Group.*

Table 6.1: Copyright Oxford University Press, 2002. Reprinted with the permission of Oxford University Press, Pakistan from their publication entitled Faithlines: Muslim Conceptions of Islam and Society *by Riaz Hassan.*

Table 6.3: Copyright Oxford University Press, 2002. Reprinted with the permission of Oxford University Press, Pakistan from their publication entitled Faithlines: Muslim Conceptions of Islam and Society *by Riaz Hassan.*

Every effort has been made to contact copyright holders. If any have been inadvertently overlooked the publishers will be pleased to make the necessary arrangements at the first opportunity.